Dad, Here's What I Really Need from You

DR. MICHELLE WATSON

HARVEST HOUSE PUBLISHERS
EUGENE, OREGON

Unless otherwise indicated, all Scripture quotations are from The Holy Bible, New International Version®, NIV®. Copyright © 1973, 1978, 1984, 2011 by Biblica, Inc.® Used by permission. All rights reserved worldwide.

Verses marked NLT are from the Holy Bible, New Living Translation, copyright © 1996, 2004, 2007 by Tyndale House Foundation. Used by permission of Tyndale House Publishers, Inc., Carol Stream, Illinois 60188. All rights reserved.

Verses marked MSG are from The Message. Copyright © by Eugene H. Peterson 1993, 1994, 1995, 1996, 2000, 2001, 2002. Used by permission of NavPress Publishing Group.

Cover design by Left Coast Design, Portland, Oregon

Cover photo © asife / Shutterstock

The author is represented by MacGregor Literary, Inc.

DAD, HERE'S WHAT I REALLY NEED FROM YOU
Copyright © 2014 by Michelle Watson
Published by Harvest House Publishers
Eugene, Oregon 97402
www.harvesthousepublishers.com

Library of Congress Cataloging-in-Publication Data
Watson, Michelle
Dad, here's what I really need from you / Dr. Michelle Watson.
pages cm
ISBN 978-0-7369-5840-0 (pbk.)
ISBN 978-0-7369-5842-4 (eBook)
1. Fathers and daughters—Religious aspects—Christianity. I. Title.
BV4529.17.W38 2014
248.8'421—dc23

2013043570

Printed in the United States of America

14 15 16 17 18 19 20 21 22 23 / LB-CD / 10 9 8 7 6 5 4 3 2 1

CONTENTS

Part Three—Dialing In to Her Heart Needs

Part Four—Under the Foundation: Looking Deeper at Yourself

FOREWORD

The economics of fathering, more specifically fatherlessness, is a topic that has received no small attention. Recent data estimates a figure of 100 billion dollars annually as the cost of fatherlessness. This a significant sum, but it does not include the staggering emotional, moral, and "loss of potential" costs that plague a child when they don't have a dad.

Conservatively, 25 million children under the age of eighteen don't live with their dad, which means roughly 12.5 million daughters go to bed tonight in a home without their father. Add to that the number of children who live with their dad but aren't connected to him relationally, emotionally, or spiritually. Therein is a much clearer picture of the true costs of fatherlessness.

Enter Dr. Michelle Watson. When I first met Michelle, I was greatly encouraged that another skilled and competent leader had been prompted to focus on strengthening father-daughter relationships. After many discussions, it was clear that Dr. Watson was a thoughtful leader who was bringing attention to the importance of those relationships.

While the costs and consequences of fatherlessness have been described in great detail in the literature, the benefits and assets created by "father*full*-ness" have been less so. The absence of a father leaves a child at risk, with hopelessness and disaster waiting in the wings. But the presence of a dad, particularly one who is responsible and humble, can breathe hope and life into a child. Remarkably, the research and opinion leaders are unified: fathers matter, and they play an essential role in healthy child development.

What impresses me most about Dr. Watson is that she recognizes how much fathers matter. Add to that her passion to see dads and daughters connect in ways that yield benefits to both, and you have fatherfullness in motion. In addition, Dr. Watson understands that reciprocity and appreciating male-female differences is the foundation for healthy relationships. Her book will help you lay the groundwork for a healthy family. Her insights are spot on.

For several years Dr. Watson has tested the efficacy of her research in small groups. She has put scores of dads through enriching and, at times, challenging training that has helped them grow in their commitment as fathers. That's right. A female, Dr. Watson, has been teaching dads with great success, and the results have been extraordinary. And how did that happen?

First, Michelle is a daughter. She knows, through an imperfect though healthy relationship with her dad, why the father-daughter relationship is so important. When you know from experience how valuable the bond between dads and daughters really is, and then are challenged to make that relationship the best it can be, a quality is added to your clinical training that supersedes the academic credential.

Second, Dr. Watson is a successful therapist. Her entire vocational career has been committed to helping women and men mature. She is licensed and has endured the scrutiny of other counseling professionals. She practices with excellence, and her case loads are always full.

Third and most important, Dr. Watson is a lifelong learner. From our first meeting and throughout the years, I have come to know that one of Michelle's gifts is wisdom. That wisdom has been tempered and shaped by another Father. The fact that she can integrate spiritual truths and realities into her training gives her a unique perspective.

I have been working in the field of fatherhood and family formation for over twenty-five years. It is always a delight to meet leaders who have discernment with respect to the fathering role. Dr. Watson is one of those. I applaud her efforts, her work, and her success in providing fresh insights to fathers and daughters. I highly recommend her book and her work as an author, a speaker, and an emerging leader.

Ken R. Canfield, PhD
Founder, National Center for Fathering
www.fathers.com

INTRODUCTION

Wayne is one of those men you don't easily forget. His six-foot-three frame carries with it a commanding presence that lets you know he's going to shoot straight whether you agree with him or not. But he also exudes a warmth and genuineness that draws people to him. As an ingenious entrepreneur, Wayne has worked hard to get where he is, and if you were to spend even five minutes with him, you would soon discover that he thrives on meeting challenges head-on and seeing them come to a positive resolution. Thus, it should come as no surprise to hear about his increasing frustration and sense of defeat when he first contacted me about joining The Abba Project, the group I lead for dads who have daughters in their teens and twenties.

As a father to two sons and one twenty-two-year-old daughter, Wayne was finally at the point of admitting that there was a disconnect between the success he was experiencing at work and his "success" as a dad. He came desperate for help to reach his daughter's heart, knowing that the time was now or never.

Wayne describes his daughter, Samantha, as "a strong-willed young lady who unfortunately has walked down the wrong path." And while conceding that "parenting is doing the best you can," Wayne was also eager to look at the ways his anger had contributed to his daughter's pain. He was ready to make amends and focus on rebuilding the bridge to her heart.

Wayne jumped in full steam ahead and enthusiastically engaged Sam in *all* homework assignments month after month. After going through the first date questionnaire (see the appendix) with her, he said: "We spent four to five hours talking. That's the longest I've ever spent with my daughter without being in an airplane!"

Once he made the decision to purposely pursue his daughter, he was fully committed, whether or not she responded to him favorably. He focused on doing his part while leaving the outcome to God. Wayne tells of the day he put a "Do Not Disturb" sign on his office door and spent *three hours* writing a letter to Sam. And once it was finished, he hired a calligrapher to rewrite it so it could be framed as a gift to her. It was heartwarming to hear him say "my letter brought her to tears."

At the end of our nine-month Abba Project journey, not only was this dad-daughter relationship strengthened, but this dad was changed. Wayne now tells stories of their newfound connection and speaks with a gentle softness in his tone that wasn't there at the start. He is proud of himself for the hard work he put in, as well he should be. But equally important has been the transformative impact on Sam's life as a result of her dad's **intentional** and **consistent** pursuit of her heart (these are two themes that you'll hear repeated throughout this book so lock them in now).

Wayne describes in his own words what being a part of The Abba Project was like for him:

Wayne's Story

> I came to the class punching and swinging—not kicking and screaming, but close. This has been a 180. My relationship with my daughter has changed. She is opening up more now, and for the first time has asked me what I thought about a guy. She has been able to see me live it out. It has been ten years of "hard," but now her heart has changed; so has mine.
>
> Michelle, you have developed your passion into a wonderful life-altering challenge for men. There are many things I will take away, many things I have already incorporated, and many more things I have yet to discover.

Sam would tell you that she wouldn't be where she is now had it not been for her dad turning his heart toward hers. She is the beneficiary of her dad's incredible, loving investment in her, and she is forever grateful.

Yes, I do understand that we as daughters are complex and complicated. And because we often don't understand ourselves, we don't make it easy on you dads to try to figure us out. No wonder John Gray wrote his book, *Men Are from Mars, Women Are from Venus.* We really are from two different planets.

Being a woman and a leader of women, I have years of experience that qualify me to guide you through the maze of being a dad to a daughter. I respect you for your willingness to learn in this forum. And now that you've heard Wayne's story, I'm hopeful that you'll let me lead the way for you too. I know it can be hard for any man to give up control, but I really think that if you trust me to lead the way, you'll be glad you did. I promise I won't bite. And for the record, weeping is optional!

But don't just take Wayne's word for it. Here's how other dads describe in one word the benefit of The Abba Project:

- life-changing
- revealing
- challenging
- positive
- eye-opening
- educational
- foundational

I want your relationship with your daughter to be strengthened so that the next generation of women is stronger and healthier than the current one. This is where I have to tell you boldly that **it's up to you to turn your heart toward hers** so she can be all that she was created to be.

I've heard many dads say that it's both terrifying and wonderful to be a father to a daughter. I get that. I would feel it too if I were in your shoes. We'll take it one step at a time. I will help you succeed as a dad. I know that we can be a great team.

PART ONE

Laying the Foundation for Heart Pursuit

CHAPTER 1

WHAT'S THIS WHOLE THING ABOUT ANYWAY?

I'm so excited that you opened this book. Whether you're a dad, a mom, a daughter, a friend, or family member who is invested in seeing dads become more active participants in their daughters' lives, I welcome you to this conversation.

You, Dad, Are a Key to Her Heart

If you're a dad, you may be wondering how a total stranger, and a woman no less, can speak to your relationship with your daughter. Hang in there and I believe this question will be answered as you see positive results from putting the resources presented here into practice. Without a doubt, you are one of the central keys to your daughter growing, changing, and becoming all that she can be.

As my friend Dr. Ken Canfield, founder of the National Center for Fathering, says, "Your role as a father is indeed one of the most important jobs you will ever have. And no one but you can activate that role in the unique way you are privileged to do."

Let me begin by asking a few questions:

- Do you happen to have a gift sometimes for saying exactly the wrong thing at the wrong time to your daughter?
- Do you ever sit across the table from her and have no idea what to say next?
- Do you love your daughter with all your heart but wonder if she knows that it's true?
- Do you find it harder to relate to her as she gets older and becomes more intriguingly complex?

If you answered yes to any of these questions, then this book might be exactly what you need. Based on feedback I've received from other dads, you want *straightforward input that both educates and inspires*. You want *pragmatic solutions that work*. You want *real stories from real men* who have made changes and seen positive impact in their relationships with their daughters.

If this strikes a chord with you, then let's get started.

Do Men Read These Kinds of Books?

A friend in the book business recently told me that 86 percent of books sold are bought by women. This confirmed that I don't want to write a book for men that looks like every other book on the shelf that men never read. The truth is that it is worth your time to read this book only if it makes a difference and helps you fix, improve, or build a stronger relationship with your daughter.

Why You Should Read This Book Even Though You Don't Really Want To

1. *Your daughter needs you,* more than you may know. These resources will help you decode her and relate even better with her.
2. *You need your daughter.* Because she touches a place in your heart that no one else can, your heart needs to open and stay open. You will both grow as a result.
3. *Your confidence will build* if you have the tools to help you connect better with her.
4. *Now is the time to dial in with more precision than ever before.* Every day that you delay investing in your daughter's heart and life is a day you can't get back.
5. *Your daughter will reach her full potential only if she has your full support and full belief in her.* If you want to leave a positive legacy, now is the time to pursue your daughter's heart.

This book will help you to reach these goals.

One more foundational point. In numerous conversations I've had with dads, most tell me they have "a great relationship" with their daughters. There seems to be a universal theme of positive assessment among fathers in this area. Yet it is equally common for me to hear the daughters of those same fathers tell me they're not very close to their dads, often with tears streaming down their faces.

I fully believe that neither side is lying, in denial, or seeking to misrepresent the relationship. Instead, I've come to understand that men and women simply have different definitions of *close.*

Dad-Daughter Disconnect

This fact was confirmed in a 2004 national poll of 424 dads and stepdads with daughters under the age of eighteen. This study was the first of its kind to assess the condition of father-daughter relationships in our country. The researchers discovered that three-fourths of the fathers surveyed believed their relationships with their daughters were "good" or "excellent" while two-thirds of them confidently stated that they "could address difficult issues" with their girls, such as sex and sexuality. However, a nonprofit group, Dads and Daughters (DADs), conducted an unscientific online survey of daughters at the same time this study was released, and three-fourths of the daughters reported they had a "poor" or "unsatisfactory" relationship with their dad. These results point to the prevalent disparity between a father's self-perception and the perspectives held by his daughter.

Dads Are "Our Greatest Untapped Natural Resource"

My deep desire is to help fathers build and strengthen the bridge to their daughter's heart. Why? Because, says Joe Kelly, cofounder of DADs, "Fathers are the key to a daughter's well-being, healthy development, and resilient self-image…and **our greatest untapped natural resource**." I love this description of you dads. This really is who you are.

Several years ago I started meeting with small groups of dads with essentially one goal: *To equip them to dial in to their daughters in more effective ways and then see if there was a subsequent change in their daughters, themselves, and their relationship as a result.* As I said earlier, I call this The Abba Project, and over time these groups have grown. We meet once a month over the course of nine months to talk about issues their daughters face, coupled with thematic monthly assignments and scripted questions they ask their daughters in order to open up deeper dialogue. This isn't a quick fix. It requires a long-term commitment.

This Isn't a Quick Fix; It's a Long-Term Commitment

I can confidently say that every dad, without exception, who has been willing to walk this journey and invest himself fully in the process has found the impact on his relationship with his daughter to be beyond what he ever could have imagined.

The following story from one of The Abba Project participants is just one out of dozens that I could have shared with you. As you can see, Andy began the project desperate for help.

Andy's Story

My name is Andy. I'm a straightforward guy and I don't need much to make me happy. I've been a firefighter for thirty-five years and am close to retirement. I am happily married and the father of five—four sons and my youngest, seventeen-year-old Meghan.

Meghan has been giving me fits for years. For some reason we tend to butt heads a lot more than I ever did with my boys. I'm at my wit's end. Everything I do seems to make her more and more angry with me. I try to talk to her, but she ends up either yelling at me or putting up walls where she won't talk to me despite my trying to open up a conversation.

I attempt to connect with her and sometimes it seems like it's better if I just say nothing at all so that I don't incite her wrath. I am convinced I'm just making it worse. If there was a way to exit stage left, I would do it. I'm honestly at a loss at this point.

I've only got eight more months with her in the house. On one hand, I'm done. But on the other, I really don't want it to end this way before she heads out on her own. I'd like to join your group if you still have room. I look forward to hearing back from you. Thanks, Andy.

Terminally Male

Andy is a full-bore "man's man." I'll never forget the night his cell phone started ringing midway through the group meeting. Suddenly one of the other dads asked, "Is your ring tone an elk call?" Sure enough, it was! Andy usually had all of us laughing uproariously with his sincere inability to understand women, prompting the suggestion from the guys to get him a shirt with "Terminally Male" on the front. All this to say, if Andy could learn to be a dialed-in dad, so can you.

Men Hate to Feel Incompetent

Andy thought he had parenting down when it came to fathering his four boys. But his confidence was at an all-time low when I first met him. And because men hate to feel incompetent, this situation with his daughter only exaggerated that fact for this frustrated dad.

Andy is like many of the dads who have been coming to my groups. He has a good heart and good intentions, yet is at the end of his rope when it comes to trying to connect with his teenage daughter. His frustration with being unable to engage her is something I am confident she feels. She then reacts by expressing anger at him for not understanding her, which prompts him to vent his anger back at her for being disrespectful. It's a lose-lose, vicious cycle.

When the relationship between a dad and his daughter goes sideways, it usually taps into a man's sense of being helpless. This oftentimes leads him to take a dominant stance using his position of authority. I've noticed that when dads are striking out with their daughters, they tend to use the *power card*. And we all know how that goes over. One word: *bomb.*

The Power Card Doesn't Work

There's a great verse in Proverbs that says "a gentle answer deflects anger" (15:1 NLT). Although this is true, dad after dad has told me that he either doesn't like the soft approach or there is no way he can pull back his anger when his daughter's emotions are escalating. (We'll talk more about this later because a dad *has to take the lead* in de-escalating himself emotionally, or healing the relationship with his daughter won't happen.)

A Soft Answer Works Wonders

Perhaps you're not one to explode, but instead are a dad who *backs up, backs down,* and *shuts down*. Maybe you're so exhausted and tired of the fight that you have now disengaged from connecting with your daughter at all. *Checkmate. Game over.*

These are common dad-daughter dynamics, especially once a daughter hits puberty. Her meltdowns start to come more frequently, and that's when you realize you can't fix the problem as easily as when it took one kiss to make her boo-boo all better.

I'll let our friend Andy tell you in his own words how things changed in his house when he changed the way he interacted with Meghan.

More of Andy's Story

When I came to your group, Michelle, I wasn't expecting a whole lot. Yet I was so desperate for any tool to help our relationship that I was willing to drive an hour each way just to attend the group. At first it was a bit uncomfortable to sit there with other men I didn't know. But the fact that we were all there simply out of love for our daughters gave us a common denominator. At least we could connect over that one thing.

I'll never forget the day you taught us to add the words "I'm wondering" when asking our daughters a question. Prior to that, I had often said to Meghan, "Why didn't you go to school today?" I was always met with no answer. Her wall immediately would go up, hostility oozing out of her. I hated it and yet had no idea how to change it.

So I went home and the very next day we had the exact same scenario, but this time I asked her, "Meghan, I'm wondering...why didn't you go to school today?" To my complete surprise, she turned to me and answered my question. I couldn't believe it. I was mostly surprised that such a simple change in me made her open up so differently with me. That tool right there was worth the price of admission.

This group has truly changed me and my relationship with my daughter. I can't thank you enough.

Like Andy, you want a fix that works. You want to see results that lead to change. But in order for this to happen, you'll have to be willing, *with everything you've got,* to enter this complex, confusing, unpredictable, amazing, and profound journey of fathering your daughter *by first looking at yourself.* If you're willing to be challenged to find out what your daughter *really* wants from you, dad, then read on.

CHAPTER 2

ON YOUR MARK, GET SET...ACTION

Here is my manifesto: *I believe that a dad investing in his daughter's life has the power to positively impact our culture like nothing else I know of.* And I am convinced, both from personal experience and extensive supporting research, that if a dad gets on board with his daughter by intentionally and consistently pursuing her heart, it will change not only both of them, but it will change our world as we know it today.

I believe in the transformative, healing power of a dad's love expressed through consistent pursuit of his daughter's heart. And I have seen that when a dad gives focused attention to his daughter by dialing into her life, life-changing, powerful, and dramatic changes occur beyond anything expected or imagined.

Being a Real-Life Action Figure

I want *you* to be the action hero that you *want* to be and that your daughter *needs* you to be. **The key ingredient is action.** And if you're anything like the dads I've interacted with, you're ready to strengthen your relationship with your daughter and are hungry for the tools to make that happen, but you're not always sure what to do. I am inspired by dads like you. My part is to give you what you need to succeed. Your part is to put the plan into action.

This will be hard work, but like any worthwhile project, **the harder the work, the greater the value. And the harder the work, the greater the reward.**

> ***Just remember:*** the most important part in all of this is turning your *heart* (not just your head) toward your daughter.
>
> It's not about being perfect. It's about being present.

You Get to Write the Playbook

Because your daughter didn't come into the world with a playbook, *you* will be writing the playbook as *she teaches you* about herself through your talks with her. As we walk through this dad-daughter strengthening process, I want you to feel as if I'm right there with you, coaching you just as I do with the dads I lead in Portland, Oregon.

For starters, here's a bit of what you can expect as we head into this journey together while you *work* (be sure to hold on to that word) to enhance your relationship with your daughter:

- topics that relate to girls and young women
- information (practical, relevant, and sound)
- interactive materials to open up dialogue with her
- insights about men and dads to increase self-awareness
- facts and truths from other notable authors
- personal stories from both dads and daughters

I've discovered that dads often underestimate how significant their role is to their daughters, particularly when they hit adolescence. (The operative word here is *hit*. You know what I'm talking about as you remember the abrupt impact to your life and hers when she went from a little girl to a young lady overnight.)

I'm Shouting from the Rooftops: Dads Matter!

Your positive, invested role as her dad is vital to her health and well-being. It will enable her to become a strong, capable, wise, and empowered woman.

I know there are myriads of books on the market about being a better dad. But we don't need more books telling us what to think. In fact, if this book merely adds to your head knowledge and sits on the shelf of your office (or even the "shelf of your mind"), I will be sorely disappointed.

This is an action book. And because knowledge without action is hollow, I want to lovingly yet boldly nudge you to action.

Clay's Story

Clay came to our group on the first night saying, "I'm really not looking forward to all the talking I'm going to have to do." This prompted another dad to remark, "Isn't that why we're doing this?" Convicted. Having one biological daughter and two stepdaughters, Clay was often overwhelmed with the female dynamics and all the talking that swirled around him. But he chose to come and learn and grow.

Clay's oldest daughter, Julia (age twenty-four), was in Haiti during the year our group met. So when he went to visit her during spring break, he brought his Abba Project notebook with him, his questions in hand, as a way to open up deeper dialogue. He said that one day they walked on the beach and wept together as she began to tell him things she had never told him before. Julia shared that after the divorce, she was always afraid he would abandon her. Clay was shocked because in his mind he had always been there for her and had no idea she felt that way.

Clay made it safe for his adult daughter to open up. *When a dad gently initiates conversation, his daughter will follow his lead.*

My Dad and I Bonk Heads, but We've Made It

As we make this journey together, I'm going to open up about my relationship with my dad as well. He and I have a solid relationship, but we've also had significant times of misunderstanding and head-bonking. I'm strong-willed and so is he. I'll let you imagine how that's played out over the last five decades! Let me sum it up by saying that *if he and I have been able to make our relationship work, there's hope for every one of you.*

So I come to this topic of fathering from a unique vantage point, not only as the oldest of four girls (my poor dad was doused with a lot of estrogen in our house), but as a woman who has been interacting in the lives of girls and young women for over thirty-five years. I will be giving you *the inside scoop* on what we girls think and feel, as well as what we *really want* from you, our dads.

I Want to Help Decode Your Daughter to You

I *really do want* you to succeed in your role as a dad. I understand girls very well as a result of delving into the dramatic heights and murky depths of life with them over the years. Girls make sense to me. And my desire is to help decode them to you so that your daughter makes a bit more sense to you. And I'm hopeful that you'll agree with one of the dads who joined me in this journey who said, "If I was given the choice, I would rather take advice from a woman than from a man about how to connect with my daughters."

And though I have written this material to apply most specifically to girls in their teens and twenties, it's an excellent foundation for dads who have younger daughters. By soaking in this material while your daughter is young, you'll lay a solid foundation to better navigate her teenage years and beyond.

Commit to Going the Distance

I want to challenge you here at the onset of this journey to commit to going the distance so that you end as strongly as you begin. If you build up your daughter's hopes by starting to engage and then stop, she will experience the words of Proverbs 13:12, "Hope deferred makes the heart sick." Girls internalize rejection very easily, and when something starts strong and then fizzles out, they interpret this as being something negative about them. **Your daughter will believe she isn't worth the investment if you pursue her but then lose enthusiasm.**

As you embark on this journey to become a dialed-in dad, I suggest that you find other like-minded men and go through this material together. There is unbelievable power in a band of brothers joining the same team. I also highly recommend that you *read this book with a pen in hand.* I know it can be easy to let information go in one ear and out the other (because I've done it more times than I can count). My hope is that this book will be different from others you've read because of how you interact with the content. But this will happen only if it becomes a *heart* book and not just a *head* book.

Make This Book Your Own

Make this *your* workbook—write in the margins, highlight things you agree or disagree with, and jot down questions and thoughts that come to mind as you read. This will then provide a personal resource for dialogue with your daughter, wife, or another dad.

The Best Way to Get the Biggest Results from This Book

- Keep a pen in hand as you read.
- *Write* in the margins.
- Answer the questions.
- Interact by agreeing or disagreeing with what you read.
- Use this material as a springboard for opening up dialogue with your wife, daughter, or other dads.
- Take the ideas, personalize them, and make them your own.
- *Write* down what you figure out along the way.
- *Write* down what you learn about your daughter...about yourself... about life. (Remember: *Write the playbook.*)

I'm sure you noticed that I used the word *write* several times in the above list. This is because your own points of awareness and individual notes will be even more memorable than anything I teach you. I realize it's not a typical guy thing to take notes in a book, but if you do, you will capture the full benefit of this experience.

Writing Increases Retention

If you're ready to actively engage your daughter's heart with more intention and consistency, then this is the book for you. You, dad, breathe life into your daughter in a way that no one else ever can, and we'll work together to build the confidence and skill set you need to enhance her life.

Now here is the first of many self-reflective questions I'll be asking you to ponder throughout this expedition. You will gain the most from this book by answering these short questions at the end of each chapter.

I'm ready to take action today in an even greater way in my daughter's life by...

(Make your action step simple, practical, and measurable.)

CHAPTER 3

BECOME A DIALED-IN DAD

Here at the starting line is the time to be honest with yourself about where you are with your daughter. I encourage you to take the time right now to go through this self-assessment, and then again later at the end of the journey, to provide a concrete way of evaluating the changes that take place in your relationship with your daughter.

The Dialed-In Dad Self-Test

	Frequently	Occasionally	Never
1. My daughter and I go on dates.	3	2	1
2. I feel I know what's happening in her life.	3	2	1
3. I tell her my thoughts or fears about the decisions she is making...*gently.*	3	2	1
4. I get frustrated or angry with her more than I used to.	1	2	3
5. I initiate conversations about spiritual things.	3	2	1
6. It's hard to talk *with* her, so more often I talk *at* her.	1	2	3
7. I feel my daughter respects me.	3	2	1
8. I struggle to engage her in serious conversation so we mostly joke with each other.	1	2	3

Here's the Action Part I Was Talking About

9. I am home for dinner with the family most nights.	3	2	1
10. I tease her about her weight (even though I say it in jest).	1	2	3
11. I make comments about other people's weight.	1	2	3
12. Favoritism is something I grew up with, and it still plays out in the way I treat my kids.	1	2	3
13. I know and have interactions with my daughter's close girlfriends.	3	2	1
14. I know and have interactions with my daughter's close guy friends.	3	2	1
15. I attend the school activities she's involved in (sports, music, drama).	3	2	1
16. I talk down to her mother, sometimes in front of my daughter.	1	2	3
17. I help my daughter with her homework.	3	2	1
18. My daughter tells me about things she is learning in school and life.	3	2	1
19. My daughter opens up about things she is learning spiritually.	3	2	1
20. I can respect the areas of difference between us (beliefs/thinking) without trying to force her to believe or think the way I do.	3	2	1
21. I watch what I want on TV even if her favorite shows are on at the same time.	1	2	3
22. I have bought her an item of clothing that she really wanted "just because."	3	2	1
23. I am okay when she cries, and she is comfortable crying in front of me.	3	2	1
24. I am comfortable letting my daughter see me cry.	3	2	1

25. We have fun traditions involving the two of us.	3	2	1
26. She and I enjoy getting physically fit together.	3	2	1
27. My daughter likes hanging out with her friends at our house.	3	2	1
28. We talk openly about alcohol and drugs, and she tells me the truth about it.	3	2	1
29. We've had an honest, interactive talk (not just me lecturing) about sex.	3	2	1
30. My positive interactions with her outweigh the negative.	3	2	1
31. I can name her favorite musical artist and song right now.	3	2	1
32. I let her play her music when we're in the car.	3	2	1
33. I have gone to see her kind of movie with her.	3	2	1
34. I criticize my body openly in front of her.	1	2	3
35. I pray for her and *with* her.	3	2	1
36. I know how to get her to laugh.	3	2	1
37. I apologize, say "I'm sorry," and ask forgiveness when I have wronged her, hurt her, or crushed her spirit.	3	2	1
38. I'm okay being silly and foolish around her, even if it means being teased by her, without being defensive.	3	2	1
39. I speak the truth in love when I communicate with her.	3	2	1
40. I use anger as a way to quiet and discipline her.	1	2	3
41. I use time in the car to lecture her.	1	2	3

42. I affirm and compliment her mom in front of her.	3	2	1
43. I handwrite her notes to tell her I love her and am thinking about her.	3	2	1
44. I text my daughter to check in and to tell her I love her and am thinking about her.	3	2	1
45. I intentionally engage her in conversation after my workday.	3	2	1
46. I compliment my daughter on her personality and character.	3	2	1
47. I let her know she looks beautiful (with words, written or verbal).	3	2	1
48. I am careful to speak positives to her (being proud of her, affirming her).	3	2	1
49. I meet the guys she dates before she goes out with them.	3	2	1
50. I am comfortable expressing physical affection to my wife in front of her.	3	2	1
51. I am comfortable expressing physical affection to my daughter.	3	2	1
52. I have spoken with my daughter about how to save and spend money.	3	2	1
53. I participate in community service with her.	3	2	1
54. I drive her to church, entering into spiritual practices *with* her.	3	2	1
55. I answer her questions without defensiveness when she asks me about my own life.	3	2	1
56. I ask questions to draw her out and keep the dialogue going.	3	2	1
57. I tell my daughter what I am learning (from books, the Bible, work, life).	3	2	1

58. I check my daughter's Internet and phone history to know where she's at.	3	2	1
59. I enter her room (with permission) just to touch base and see the lay of her land.	3	2	1
60. I have a pattern of checking in with her and just listening.	3	2	1
Total each column			
My total score is			

Scoring Template

Time for Some Self-Assessment

170-180: I am strongly tuned in to my daughter's life while consistently pursuing her heart.

140-169: Overall I am dialed in, but some areas need my attention and commitment to improve.

110-139: It's hit or miss in terms of intentionally investing in my daughter's life. I admit my shortcomings here without making excuses. It's time to kick it up a notch.

60-109: I have fallen short of being a solid role model. Change has to begin with me if I want to win back my daughter's trust and actively engage in healing her wounded heart.

If you're like the men in my groups, you're ready to use your score both as a gauge for where you are now as well as a guide for where you still need to focus. I've loved hearing dads in The Abba Project tell me that they made a copy of this self-test and put it in a prominent place to remind them of what they need to work on.

Committed over the Long Haul

Speaking of prominent places, I was blown away when Police Chief Bret, a former Abba Project Dad, sent me a picture a year after our group ended. Placed next to his bulletproof vest, leather belt, and two guns was his Abba Project notebook, propped up as a daily reminder of the importance of investing in his three daughters. He wanted me to see that he wasn't forgetting to dial in even after our group ended. Way to go, dad.

Let's get practical now.

As you look back over the Dialed-In Dad Self-Test and see items that are not a part of your daily or weekly interactions with your daughter, write out two or three specific things (in the box below) that you are going to do starting today that will launch you on your journey toward being a more tuned-in, dialed-in dad.

There's no need to go down a path of guilt or shame for things you've done wrong in the past, and *there's no better time than the present to begin changing the past.* You have today and every day from here on out to make up for lost time.

Results from Abba Project Dads

There's nothing like a good statistic to reinforce a truth. Here are some numbers I've gathered from dads who have completed The Abba Project journey with me. Their before-and-after results speak for themselves. After nine months of intentional focus on fathering:

- 71 percent of dads started going on dates with their daughters
- 53 percent began to engage in more serious conversations
- 23 percent reported more ease with their daughter's tears
- 31 percent learned her favorite musical artist and song
- 18 percent asked forgiveness after having wronged, hurt, or crushed her spirit
- 18 percent grew in knowing what was happening in her life

Here's the bottom line: **Being intentional makes a big difference.**

Challenge yourself to choose a couple of new ways to connect with your daughter as you go forward on this journey. Use lower-scoring items on the Dialed-In Dad Self-Test to guide you here.

Starting today I will actively pursue my daughter's heart by...

1.

2.

3.

CHAPTER 4

DECODING YOURSELF FIRST

Here's something I've discovered about men: **Men would rather do nothing than do it wrong.**

This conclusion comes from three decades of interacting with men in various contexts and also seeing how dads tend to interact with their daughters once puberty sets in and things get way more complicated. *Sound familiar?*

The good news is that by reading the questions I give you to ask your daughter (see the appendix), you can't do it wrong. If it works, then you'll succeed because she'll talk. And if it bombs, you can blame me and I'll be your "fall guy"!

Seriously though, if you read the scripts I give you for your dad-daughter dates (more about these at the end of the next chapter), and then listen and engage with her, you will see that the words I put into your mouth will help you to open up dialogue in ways that are probably different than they've been before. Your confidence will increase as your daughter responds positively and you get it right.

Think of This as Being in Language School

Because women are from Venus and men are from Mars, it's not your fault that you haven't been able to figure out yet how to speak Venusian with your daughter. And though you may not have thought of this as a journey where you're attending language school, that's actually what you're signing up for! And because I speak fluent Venusian, I'm going to teach you how to speak your daughter's native tongue.

In all actuality, *your daughter will teach you how to speak her native language.* Every girl has her very own dialect (which those of you with more than one daughter know all too well), and she will teach you how to converse with her if you're willing to learn. I'm simply here as your interpreter to help the process along.

I know that dads often grow weary of trying to navigate the mercurial years of their daughters' adolescence and young adulthood because girls during those years are frequently unpredictable and confusing. Dads tend to pull away during this season of life, often leaving the heavy lifting to Mom, which leaves gaping holes in the lives of their girls.

It's time to turn that around and turn toward your daughter.

What I've Discovered About Men (the short version)

Here are a few more things I've discovered that men need to engage in a project, which is a vital part of turning toward something or someone. These four things will set a foundation in beginning this journey with your daughter:

1. ***Men need a mission.*** A clear starting point is key. Tell your daughter that you are going to pursue her heart more intentionally going forward.
2. ***Men need a mindset.*** Set your mind and intention to do this consistently no matter what interferences, challenges, or resistances arise.
3. ***Men need a mouthpiece.*** Plan to engage her in dialogue by asking questions. (I'll give you exactly what you need to do this.)
4. ***Men need a miracle.*** You will need a Resource greater than yourself to do this work. Call on God to give you the strength to reach your daughter's heart.

A Toolbox Needs Tools

Another thing I know about men is that you like to fix things. Imagine for a moment that you're opening a toolbox in which you find all the tools you will need to build a stronger relationship with your daughter.

If such a toolbox existed, would you want one? Of course you would!

Now think of yourself as the *builder*, your daughter as the *house,* and me as the *architect* helping you and *"the build"* to be successful. To achieve your objective, you'll need effective tools, which I'll be giving you to fill your toolbox as we go along.

Here's how the dictionary defines *build*:

1. to construct: especially something complex
2. to establish, increase, or strengthen
3. to mold, form, or create
4. to engage in the art, practice, or business of building
5. to form or construct a plan, system of thought

6. to increase or develop toward a maximum, as of intensity, tempo, or magnitude

Putting on Your Tool Belt

Putting it all together, this means you have the opportunity to *increase* and *strengthen* the core of your daughter's self-concept by *affirming* who she is and *celebrating* her uniqueness. You get to help *mold, form,* and *shape* her identity by consistently *building her up*. As you strategically *construct a plan* to intentionally *encourage* her to be her authentic self (even if she chooses a different path than you wish or choose for her), while steadily *increasing the tempo and magnitude* of your positive input as she grows older, her ability to embrace her core identity will increase proportionately.

I know I'm giving you a lot of words, so let's take a break from the action while I share something that's a bit on the lighter side.

You'll recall me saying that 86 percent of books sold are bought by women. This statistic prompted me to conduct my own informal survey of men and their reading habits. Through this, I learned a lot about what works for men when it comes to connecting to the written word.

The Man Survey Says...

The Top 10 Things I Learned from Men About Their Reading Habits

(See if you agree with this Top 10 List as I present it David Letterman style, beginning with 10.)

10. The title has to be catchy and clever or we won't pick it up.

9. We don't like too many words.

10. We like short chapters that make us feel as if we're accomplishing something.

11. We like personal and real-life stories that keep us engaged.

12. We like a good mix of humor, statistics, pictures, and life application.

13. We like to be moved to action with baby steps toward a solution.

14. We usually like magazines better than books because the information is laid out in a way that holds our attention. (I found a 2:1 ratio of guys who read magazines more than books.)

3. The content has to be relevant and practical.

2. The writing has to be good—informative, solid, and fact based.

And the number 1 thing men say they need to stay interested in reading...

1. Get to the point already!

I can assure you that even though I'm from Venus where words run aplenty, my goal is to nail as many of these ten things as I can. But the truth is…there will be words! So maybe we'll have to compromise there.

The main thing to remember is that just by reading this book, **you're already one step closer toward building a stronger relationship with your daughter because you are open to learning and growing.**

Getting Your Purpose on Paper

To help make your goal clear from the start, take a moment and write down your mission statement in the box below. A mission statement is a declaration of purpose that clarifies a vision or a goal. Dads say that they are motivated and driven by such a statement. Examples include: "I will daily affirm my daughter for who she is, whether in person or in writing, so that she never doubts my love for her," and "Every day of my daughter's life I will deliberately seek to model God as a good father to her, starting with honoring her with the words I speak." Your statement of intention will remind you of your lifelong, ongoing "mission" with your daughter.

My hope is that by investing in your daughter through this process, you will be able to say, just like Dave, an Abba Project Dad, *"I'm glad I didn't give up. It was hard for a few months there in the middle, but now the hard work has paid off."*

When the road gets rough, you'll be able to read what you wrote in the box below and remember why you started this journey of intentionally dialing in.

My Mission Statement and the reason I am becoming a more dialed-in dad is...

CHAPTER 5

ACTIVATING YOUR HEART

A counseling mentor and friend of mine, Dr. Jim Friesen, has said the following so many times that it's now burrowed deep within me: *"We either live from our hurt or we live from our heart."*

It All Starts with the Heart

How deeply insightful these words are. When it comes to the dad-daughter relationship, many girls have been wounded or neglected, leading to her emotional wall going up. The result is girls who live from their *hurt places* rather than their *heart places*.

Yet despite past hurts from dad, most, if not all girls still long for connection with their dads. Let me give you a window into the soul longings of girls in relation to their dads:

A Window into the Heart Cries of Girls

"I gave up wanting to be close to my dad a long time ago. He doesn't seem to want to be close to me, so I don't want to be close to him either anymore."

"I wish I had more time with my dad."

"My dad is so busy and he doesn't have time for me."

"My dad thinks we're close, but we actually never talk about anything deep."

Then the tears usually start. I have seen girls cry more over the lack of relationship with their dads than over anything else. This, dads, is what fuels my passion for this project.

Whether your daughter is pushing you away or pulling you close right now, the most important thing to remember is that *as you turn your heart toward your daughter, she will turn her heart to you.* It's a reciprocal relationship. And if not right now, stay the course and believe for a miracle.

Open Conversation, Open Heart

I've interacted with countless dads who say they don't know exactly what it means to engage their hearts because they tend to "live in their heads." I tell them, as I'm telling you, that when a girl opens her mouth, her heart automatically opens. I've seen it happen a thousand times. So as you open up conversations with her (using scripts I'll give you), her heart will open up to you. And your heart, in turn, will open up to her. It's win-win.

Stated simply, **a dad's heart automatically opens when his daughter's heart engages his heart.** This is where you come in. You can be a catalyst to helping her heart open up and stay open.

Think back to when your daughter was born. Do you remember when you first laid eyes on her and felt a love you had never experienced before? Her beautiful little face captivated you as her tiny fingers wrapped around yours, and from that first moment you were smitten.

My Definition of a Real Man

That's the heart place that I'm seeking to help you connect with, the place where you feel warm, tender, engaged, and connected. This, my friend, is the true definition of being a man: one who lives from his heart while being connected to his head.

Before we go on, I want you to hear from other dads who have joined me in this journey as they describe the benefit of engaging in this process.

Voices of Dads Who Have Walked This Journey

"When my daughter hit puberty, it was like a Polynesian Island getting hit with nuclear weapons. So I came in needing all the help I could get…and I wasn't disappointed."

"She told me she was really jazzed that I'd do this just for her."

"I'm realizing that I've asked a lot of questions but just not the right type of questions to get her to open up. Now she's actually talking."

"I thought my daughter was the whole problem. But now in just one month of me doing this, the whole climate in our house has changed."

"By doing this I learned so much about her that I didn't know. The questionnaires really helped guide our conversation."

As you see here, there are no *typical* responses from dads who decide to start this undertaking. For some it has come easy and for others it's been an uphill climb. Some are rebuilding; others are getting an early start.

But in the end, I've not had a single dad regret doing this project with his daughter.

You, dad, are a key to your daughter's heart opening and staying open. And because you are vital and pivotal and necessary and important, I am thrilled to be partnering with you in this adventure.

And because the most important part of this whole journey is connecting with your daughter's heart, I want to make sure the definition of *heart* is clear.

Defining *Heart* Connections

- engaging with her at an emotional level through consistent verbal and nonverbal expressions of love
- the capacity for sympathy
- the capacity for affection
- the center of the total personality, especially with reference to intuition, spirit, and soul
- the center of emotion, especially as contrasted to the head as the center of intellect

See...it *is* all about connecting with feelings and emotions.

This means your heart has to be activated toward your daughter in a soft, gentle, kind, respectful, and emotionally engaged way if you want her to open up to you.

If You Forget Everything Else I've Said, Remember This...

Activating your heart is the most important thing to remember out of this whole book.

I'm serious. This is the crux of everything I'll be teaching you on every page. If you want your daughter's heart to turn toward you, you have to first turn your heart to her.

Daughter's heart + dad's heart = LIFE to both of you.

Daughter's heart – dad's heart = DEATH to both of you (emotionally and spiritually).

As you know, life is more enjoyable for you and for your daughter when you're getting along. Thus, when the alliance between you is strengthened, both of you reap the benefits. So what do you have to lose by engaging in this process?

Nothing to Lose, Everything to Gain

The answer: Nothing. You have only a daughter's heart to gain.

Don't give up no matter what obstacles come your way. It's worth it in the end. Although you may want to demand that your daughter open her heart to you (especially during her teens and twenties when it's often more of a challenge to connect), you'll have to *pace with her* based on where she is with you, with her life, and with herself.

Listen again to what other dads just like you are saying as time passes quickly and their little girls grow up faster than they thought possible. These dads have dialed in regardless of what has passed under the bridges in their relationships with their daughters. Their stories underscore that *now* is the time to engage with your daughter. There's no better time than the present to pursue her heart.

Dads Looking Back

"I wish I would have known this when my daughter was younger."

"I've needed more tools because what I've been doing clearly hasn't been working."

"It's amazing how little I know. I just hope that I haven't started too late."

"Why did I have to wait this long to start learning this stuff?"

One of my very favorite comments came from Rick, who said at the end of our Abba Project year, "Through this process I not only have become a better dad to my daughter, but also to my two sons. I'm even a better husband to my wife, *and* a better manager at work. These principles have really changed things." If this doesn't encourage you to stay the course, I'm not sure what will.

This really is about changing the lives of daughters, but I keep hearing dads say that *they* are the ones who are changing for the better.

And now it's your turn to take something from this chapter and make it practical and action packed.

The one way I am going to intentionally, proactively, and clearly express my heart of love to my daughter today is...

Initiating Dad-Daughter Dates

One key component to being a dialed-in dad, one who takes action in order to be the hero you want to be and that your daughter wants you to be is to initiate regular dad-daughter dates. I use the word *regular* to give you freedom to choose the frequency based on your and your daughter's schedules. I recommend that you initiate a date once a month at the very least. Most often I've heard Abba Dads say they have chosen an informal, casual setting for their dates, but many of them have enjoyed surprising their girls periodically with an extra special restaurant destination. These dates will create positive memories that your daughter will treasure forever. I know because I have similar memories with my dad.

The purpose of your dad-daughter date isn't simply to *do* something together (as is often the case when dads and sons spend time together); the purpose is to intentionally structure the date around communicating. Most girls bond, connect, and thrive when their relationship with their dad includes freedom of expression, where you hear what she has to say while sharing things about yourself as well. It's your job as her dad to make her feel safe and loved enough to want to share her thoughts and feelings with you.

The appendix includes eight Dad-Daughter Date Questionnaires that will provide you with scripts to assist in creating deeper dialogue between you and your daughter. Each questionnaire corresponds to chapters in the book while addressing a different theme, such as dating, body image, and spiritual issues. I will tell you which questionnaire to take with you on each of your eight dates as you go along.

The first questionnaire is the longest (thirty-two questions) and is intended for you to have options for your initial date based on topics you know your daughter will enjoy talking about. My goal with this first set of questions is to start things out in a fun and lighthearted way. Enjoy!

See the appendix for "Date 1: Dad to Daughter Questions."

CHAPTER 6

THINKING BACKWARD

If you've ever played sports (which I assume includes all of you in one way or another), you know that every single time you step onto the field or court, you always know where the goal is. *Always.* The goal has *everything* to do with the direction you run, the points you make (or miss), and whether you win or lose.

The energy you expend is always oriented toward the goal because that's where the points are. That's what counts.

Without a clear goal, you can't *play* the game.

Without a clear goal, you can't *win* the game.

With your daughter, it's the same way.

What Is Your Goal?

As you think about "the game you're playing" (I'm using *game* as a metaphor to capture the essence of the interpersonal dynamic between the two of you, not as something fake in your relationship), *are you clear about the goal you have in your relationship with her?*

I can't think of too many dads who are clear about the goal or outcome they are shooting for with their daughter. Maybe a general idea, but not a specific goal. And for a goal to work, *it has to be clear, specific, measurable, and achievable.*

Leaving a Legacy

Have you taken the time to honestly and directly state for yourself your goals as a dad with your daughter? This goes hand in hand with your earlier mission statement where you wrote your purpose on paper. Now you can add an additional piece where you are even clearer and more specific. Then you'll know what you're aiming for as a dad, and when you look back, you can evaluate whether you've hit your target in reaching your precious daughter's heart.

My Three Clear, Specific, Measurable, and Achievable Goals as I Pursue My Daughter Are...

1.

2.

3.

I'm going to add one more layer to this concept of goal setting with your daughter. I call it *thinking backward.*

This time I recommend that you think about not just the here and now, but also about the future. It can be a new way of looking at the present by imagining the end of your life and thinking backward from then to now. I'm not trying to be morbid. Just stating a reality that we all have to face.

We All Leave an Imprint

We all leave a legacy. One way or another, we leave an imprint. So I invite you to ask yourself a tough question, one that will allow you to be brutally honest with yourself while sitting in the reality that you are leaving a legacy for good or bad, whether you want to or not.

What do you want your legacy to look like? For real.

She Will Carry You with Her

You will literally change the course of history through your active engagement with your daughter at the *heart level.* She will carry you with her after you leave this earth. Your legacy will live on through your daughter in proportion to your *heart investment* in her.

Though you won't be around forever physically, **you will be around forever in the deposit you leave in your daughter's life.** A theory in the field of psychology claims that some adults have an internalized parent who lives on inside them. Long after that parent is gone, the adult child may still seek to please the parent who is no longer around to see the performance.

Sadly, many adults aren't free to be who God created them to be because they are still trying to live up to the expectations of a deceased parent. I continually hear heartbreaking stories that support that fact, not only from hurting women but from discouraged husbands as well. This underscores the importance of taking the time *now* to decide what legacy you want to leave for your daughter.

Carefully consider the following statement, and then finish the sentence in your own words.

At the end of my life, if my daughter had only one thing to say about me, I'd want it to be...

Looking at the response you just wrote, *is it a head response or a heart response?* I *know* you wrote a heart response. *How do I know that?* Because every dad I've ever invited to finish this sentence has written a heart response.

Here are some of the things I've heard dads say they hope their daughters would say about them at the end of their lives:

What a Dad Wants to Hear

"There isn't anything he wouldn't do or give for me, even at a cost to himself."

"I never doubted his love for me."

"I knew he adored me."

"He loved the Lord with all his heart and soul, and he loved me in the same way."

I've heard it said that men do best when they're challenged. And not just challenged to do something possible, but something bigger and harder than they could ever imagine doing. Case in point: I just saw a documentary where men voluntarily attended a week of grueling military boot camp, paying large sums of money to be pushed past their limits. *Why did they do it?* They said it was simply to prove that they could.

Plan for the Long Haul

Well, dad, the challenge before you is to engage your daughter's heart... consistently and intentionally. And in like fashion to the demands of boot camp, here's the mindset that must be activated:

- *Over the long haul* (throughout her whole life, not just until she goes off to college or gets married)
- *Across the mountains and valleys* (her emotional ups and downs)
- *Through sleet and snow and pouring rain* (riding out the "short tear sets" to "full-court-press downpours" of emotion and irrationality)
- *Under threat of night* (staying up late to interact with her when you'd rather be in bed fast asleep)
- *Or at first morning light* (when she wakes up on the wrong side of the bed or you figure out that this is her "time of the month")

Quick Dad Tip: Speaking of her monthly cycle, here is advice from Mark, an Abba Project Dad, who learned this while living with two daughters and a wife: "When you take out the trash and see used feminine products, it's a reminder to take immediate steps to be extra sensitive so bombs don't go off." It's amazing how a little sensitivity can go a long way.

CHAPTER 7

ASSESSING FOR A HEART ATTACK

Eight-year-old Olivia and her older sister, Ali, love spending the night at my house. We do all kinds of fun, crazy things like eating ice cream at 10:00 p.m. while sitting on the front lawn with glow sticks around our necks, accessories that later become the perfect props for our dance show as we wave hello to the moon and any cars passing by. During one sleepover the girls and I were talking in the kitchen while they painted masterpieces with acrylic paint on canvas. Olivia began asking me about my job, and I said that as a counselor I help people with their *heart hurts*. Her response brought me to tears as she expressed a profound truth: "Heart hurts hurt more than physical hurts." So true.

Heart Hurts

Does your daughter have heart hurts? *Is she at risk for a heart attack?* (I'm talking, of course, about the emotional state of her heart.)

But in order to assess her heart condition, we first must define our terms. Webster says that a heart attack is "a condition in which the heart stops its normal rhythmic beating due to the supply of blood being either severely reduced (blocked) or stopped completely." Most heart attacks are the culmination of years of living with this silent but progressive disease as it wreaks havoc internally, whether or not the individual knows about it.

What impact has your relationship had, and is it currently having, on your daughter's heart? Are you willing to take an honest look at the patterns that have been set in motion over the years? As Dr. Ken Canfield says, "Awareness is a wall with windows—windows that let us look into our own soul and our child's soul."

Looking at Patterns

To look within, I invite you to honestly answer these questions:

- What is the internal condition of my daughter's heart after years of my interactions with her?
- Is her heart healthy due to the way I've helped her open it up or is it blocked so that life can't flow through it?
- Is she at risk for a heart attack due to blockages as a result of damage ("heart hurts")?

Backing It Up with Research

I've read countless articles and books on the impact a father has on his daughter. The overriding themes I've discovered from this research strongly support that children who feel connected to their fathers:

- do better in school (better grades and likely to finish high school plus attend college)
- experience greater self-esteem
- have significantly fewer suicide attempts
- have less body dissatisfaction and healthier weights
- delay having premarital sex (naturally decreases teen pregnancies)
- are more likely to find steady employment
- report less depression
- have lower rates of substance abuse (drugs and alcohol)
- display empathy and positive social behavior
- are 80 percent less likely to spend time in jail (compared to kids with uninvolved fathers)

If that doesn't lead you to dial in, you might want to check your pulse! And if you've ever questioned whether you have a profound effect on your daughter's life, this data should dispel all doubt.

A Daughter's Letter to Her Dad

The following letter is from a daughter to her dad after he accelerated his pursuit of her heart. I hope it will encourage you to do the same, whether on your own or in a forum where you are gathering with other dads to encourage each other to pursue your daughters' hearts. Your daughters will thank you.

Katie's Story

> Dear Dad,
>
> I am very thankful that you took the time this year to attend The Abba Project. It really means a ton to me that you would invest in our relationship like that—especially during one of the hardest years in our

relationship. I know it's hard to understand me, but just the effort you are making counts a whole lot.

You are a supporter of my dreams, you are a creative problem solver, you are generous, a good listener, a godly man, a loving father, tell me I'm beautiful, are okay with chick flicks, steady emotional presence, give good advice, my protector, a good husband, faithful, work on your own "stuff," honest, a good communicator, fun to be around... and you want to be around us. Thank you for handling my taxes and taking care of fees associated with it. That removed a lot of stress from my life.

Thank you for pursuing me and continuing to learn about me, for understanding I am a work in progress. Thank you for praying for me. I am excited to grow in our father-daughter relationship and our friendship in the years to come.

Love, Katie

Can you hear the numerous things in Katie's letter that tie to her heart, her emotional center? She emotionally responds with gratitude to her dad's support, generosity, listening to her (we'll get more into that later), emotional steadiness, desire to be around her, and his part in decreasing her stress by entering into her life with her. All of these are her responses to *his* initiation, *his* engagement, *his* love, and *his* pursuit of things that matter to her.

Gentle Pursuer of Her Heart

Perhaps you are in a place now with your daughter where you've seen her heart shut down as she shuts you out. She won't talk, and despite your invitations, nothing is working to open her heart to you. If this is the case, I want to implore you to be a *gentle* pursuer of her heart. I realize for most men this probably seems wimpy and anything but manly. But if you want to reach your daughter, you'll have to reach her in the way she responds best. *Tone of voice* is the biggest factor in determining whether your daughter perceives you as warm and gentle. If you look into her eyes when you talk to her, you'll be able to tell if she's pulling away or being drawn to you. But don't just take my word for it—ask her if you're coming across gentle. She will be blown away if you invite her feedback.

Girls open their hearts only when they feel safe, secure, loved, and invited. This is where they often succumb to the "bad boys" because those guys have this down to a science. For now, just know that if you gently pursue her heart and avoid harsh attacks, criticism, condemnation, force, or anger, your daughter's heart will open up in time.

Invite Without Demanding

This may sound like you're expected to be a combination of Superman, James Bond, and Jesus Himself. Yet the point here is that *if you hurt her heart, make amends*. Don't get defensive and focus on being right. Things will fall into place as your daughter sees that you are open to being honest, even when it means admitting your own shortcomings. Come humbly. She'll eventually respond. Invite without demanding.

I can think of times when my dad has admitted that his response toward me wasn't right. It meant the world to me that he would humble himself in this way, and I respect him more as a result.

When your relationship is strengthened with honest heart interactions, it will weather the minor bumps and bruises.

And if your daughter is in her teen years, just know that the dad-daughter bumps are all part of normal adolescence, as fifteen-year-old Alena so clearly expressed to her Abba Project Dad in this letter:

A Teen's Letter to Her Dad

> Dearest Daddy,
>
> Our relationship hasn't always been wonderful, but I've seen improvements this year. I've never quite realized how insightful you are and frankly, it kind of amazes me.
>
> All I really want to say is that even though I'm not always perfectly happy, and I don't always do what would please you and Mom, I wouldn't want to change the life you've made for me. I know I have a father and a family that will always love me, and that's what matters.
>
> Our family isn't always the most functional, but we're together. I hope I can grow up to have a family that's even just half as functional as ours.
>
> PS: I know I don't say this enough, but I love you.

Now it's time to bring things from your head to your heart.

Having given this some thought, my assessment of where my daughter's heart is in relation to how I've treated her is...

CHAPTER 8

TURNING YOUR HEART (NOT JUST YOUR HEAD)

When I originally got "the download" from God to start The Abba Project, it came on the heels of reading in Luke 1 where Zechariah was told that his son, John, would help "turn the hearts of fathers to their children" (v. 17 NLT). At that time, the main thing I took away from this verse was that I was being given a really amazing yet daunting assignment to help equip dads to be more intentional with their daughters.

How on Earth Do You Turn a Heart?

As time has gone on, however, I've pondered the significance of this carefully scripted and unusual wording, "turn the *hearts* of fathers." I've never had anyone ask me to "turn my heart" toward them, and I know I haven't ever asked anyone to turn their heart toward me. It's beautifully poetic and purposeful in the way it's worded, which is why I'm especially drawn to it.

A Heart Turn Is a Choice

A much more common expression is "turn the head." Turning the head is so instinctive and automatic that we don't think about it when it happens. We just do it. Turning our hearts isn't reflexive. It's directed by a decision, a choice, maybe even a passion.

For most dads it's far more natural to tune in and engage at the *head* level. Turning the heart is typically harder for a man to do.

Most girls I've known have told me they need and appreciate intellectual input from their dads. After all, it's usually dad who helps her figure out everything from filling out a FAFSA (federal student aid form) to picking the NCAA Final Four, from filling out complicated college or job applications to solving complex math problems.

But more often than not, when a daughter's lack of calm or rational perspective makes her dad feel unappreciated or disrespected, he tends to get frustrated and can blow up right then and there. Or if he doesn't get angry, at the very least his heart turns away from her. And consequently her heart shuts down. Stalemate. Checkmate.

Turned Head = Information Exchange

A turned head implies information is being exchanged. It simply means that something or someone has caught the attention of another as mental activity is stimulated. The head is the seedbed of thought and deliberation, of consideration and contemplation. It's where choice originates and decisions are birthed. We use the phrase "a meeting of the minds" to express contemplative connection with a splash of brilliance and understanding between two parties.

Yet in relation to dads and daughters, it does seem a bit formal and businesslike to think of a head-to-head connection, a brain touching a brain even if the rest of the person is less than connected.

The language in Luke 1 about a turned heart is less intuitive for men and takes more work than a turned head. I figure that God must have written this directive about a turned heart for a reason, which means not only is it possible for dads to do it, but it also must be important or He wouldn't have worded it this way. Because this language is intentional, it invites the question whether there's a difference between a dad turning his *head* and turning his *heart.*

I have no doubt that there's a vast difference between the two. Yes, a girl needs head connections with her dad in order to navigate life, *but heart connections with him are vital to her survival.* And God knows that girls have that need, which is why He worded it that way.

Turned Heart = Emotion and Connection

A turned heart implies emotion and connection. It can bypass thought, perhaps even words. It is *responsive, engaged, heartfelt,* and *receptive*. A turned heart communicates a depth of openness and availability as there is congruence between what the eyes say, the mouth speaks, and the heart expresses. It's about *authentic, open, tender, honest interaction* based on a foundation of *unconditional love and acceptance.*

And a girl can tell if her dad has his heart turned toward her or if only his head is turned.

Example: You're watching the game. It's your team against Notre Dame. Fourth quarter. Score is tied. She comes in crying. You tell her you're listening. One ear toward her. One ear toward the game. One and a half eyes on the game. Half an eye on her. Bad timing. Dilemma.

If you're serious about turning your heart, expect to be inconvenienced.

Girls have an *intuitive radar* that can read the difference between a head or a heart response. Even if she never says anything to you about it, she is constantly picking up cues and messages about herself based on these interactions with you.

Here's the truth: **men read lines and women read between the lines.**

Men tend to be straightforward and say what they mean and mean what they say. Not a lot of hidden agendas or hidden meanings. In fact, most men are exhausted just trying to keep up with all the possible meanings that women give to events, relationships, situations, themselves, outcomes, et cetera!

Women Read into Everything

Women, on the other hand, pretty much read into *everything*. This is just how we're wired. It's a DNA thing, I guess you could say, because every woman I know has this same thing going on.

We try to rise above, yet deep down we're always wondering if your tone or look or inflection or mood or stance—basically anything and everything that's going on with you—could possibly mean that you're mad or unhappy with us. Women excel at looking under, over, alongside, and through every conversation, every look, every voice inflection, and every facial expression.

When it comes to daughters and dads, daughters are constantly reading between the lines of their interactions (or lack of) with their dads. Whether there's a lot of interaction, little interaction, no interaction, reactive interaction, humorous interaction, or loving interaction, every single girl is interpreting every single interaction, good or bad, between her and her dad.

She is continually sorting out who she is and where she's going in life. **And her dad's reflection back to her about herself helps her understand and know herself better.**

Let me put it a bit more clearly...in a way that is stated *on the lines:*

So Dad... Here Are Your Lines

- If you, dad, laugh at her jokes, she tells herself, *I'm funny.*
- If you discuss politics and world events with her, she tells herself, *I'm interesting.*
- If you draw her out, asking her opinion about something, she tells herself, *I'm knowledgeable.*
- If you ask for her help to fix something, she tells herself, *I'm capable.*
- If you ask her to help you brainstorm about buying a present for her mom, she tells herself, *I'm clever.*

- If you applaud her for her achievements in sports, grades, music, or work, she tells herself, *I'm competent.*
- If you enthusiastically affirm her artistic endeavors, she tells herself, *I'm creative.*
- If you celebrate her academic prowess, she tells herself, *I'm smart.*
- If you actively listen to her while she's talking, she tells herself, *I'm engaging.*
- If you teach her to say no and then respect her boundaries, she tells herself, *I'm strong.*
- If you light up and smile when she walks into the room, she tells herself, *I'm delightful.*
- If you respect her opinions about topics ranging from literature to spiritual things, she tells herself, *I'm wise.*
- If you treat her with kindness, understanding, tenderness, and love, she tells herself, *I'm worthy.*

And on it goes. There is no end to the impact on a daughter from the messages her dad gives her. The bottom line is this:

Head interactions rest on the lines.
(predictable, factual, informative, content-driven)
Heart interactions rest between the lines.
(intuitive, connected, emotional, sensitive, heartfelt)

The clearer a dad's positive messages to his daughter, the less reading between the lines she will need to do. She will thrive as she knows and feels that her father delights in her.

Why is this? Because when a girl *feels* her dad's heart turned toward her, she believes there is nothing she can't do because her father knows best. She then is free to be all she was created to be.

A strength I have when it comes to turning my heart toward my daughter is...

An area I need to work on when it comes to turning my heart toward her is...

CHAPTER 9

A PICTURE IS *NOT* WORTH A THOUSAND WORDS

I just had a funny conversation with my dad. He was telling me that he had a forty-five-minute conversation with one of his friends today, and the first question that came out of my mouth was, *"What did you guys talk about?"*

My dad immediately became defensive and asked, "Why would you want to know that?" I was dumbfounded and gave the obvious female response, *"Because I'm from Venus and this is always what we ask when we care about someone."*

I went on to explain that most of us girls tell each other every minute detail of what our conversations with other people are about. Sometimes we tell it word for word, but always concept by concept. On our planet, it shows that we care when we ask questions and then share those details. I'm guessing that you're in good company with my dad, a guy who has been married to his wife for over fifty years and has raised four daughters. And yet, bless his Martian heart, he is still learning about life on Venus!

Words Are Vitally Important

Bottom line: Words with your girls are *very* important. They will remember your words, both your implied words and your directly stated words.

You can't bypass communicating with your daughter just because you're not in the mood or have used up all your words at work that day. If you want to really go the distance, you'll have to intentionally tank up before heading into a conversation.

She Needs You to Hear Her Words

When it comes to connecting with your daughter's heart, the reality is that she does need to hear your words. And she also needs you to hear hers. She wants and needs you to care about her spoken words and her unspoken words. She wants you to hear over and under what she is saying.

It might be easier to hear her heart if she were to say it in a letter. So here is my attempt to capture the essence of what your daughter would probably say in a letter to you.

Love Letter to Dad

Dear Dad,

I know I don't make sense a lot of the time. I wish I did. I'm not trying to make life difficult for you, I promise. It's just that sometimes everything inside me is so intense and you just get the overflow.

If I actually understood myself better, I would tell you what I need and want and think, but I don't. And when you say I don't make sense, it only makes me feel worse.

When I talk things out, I actually figure myself out...kind of. I know you aren't wired like me so you probably don't get that. But when you just let me talk and don't put me down for "being dramatic" and "over reactive," it helps me. For some reason I feel better when I get things out and you listen and are nice. Things get clearer when I hear it outside my head.

That's why I need you to be there for me when I'm having a bad day, not lecturing me but helping me stay connected to the truth of who I am on my best days...when I'm my best version of myself. It's hard for me to stay connected to that place inside myself, and I need you to help me get there. Please keep believing in me. I really do want you to be proud of me.

Love, Me

Dad, I hope you heard the heart of the message in this letter. Every girl truly wants to be her *"daddy's girl."* And sometimes she acts out if she's not getting enough positive words from you. She longs for you to validate and affirm her as your valued, precious girl...regardless of her age. (In fact, married girls still need this from their dads too.)

Relationships Fuel and Drive Us

Girls are wired to respond with their hearts and from their hearts. God made us that way. And even when we shut down and put walls up, we eventually come back to relationships because relationships are what fuel us and drive us.

We do best when our key relationships are at peace and when there is a solid connection to the people around us.

And even when we push you away, we wish the connection to you was stronger and better and more consistent. We don't want things to be off, but sometimes the reality of life boils down to this: When relationships with our friends drain the life out of us, there just isn't much left to navigate our relationship with you. We're not shutting you out on purpose. We just need you to be patient.

Look around at all the drama and energy that encircles your daughter's relationships. That's the norm for females, frankly. And girls, no matter the age, are passionate about investing in their relationships, often at a high cost to their own sanity (and yours!).

We Thrive Best in Relationally Supportive Environments

It's vital for you as a dad to grasp that *your daughter thrives best in a relationally supportive environment*, because once you understand that you will move heaven and earth to ensure that your relationship with her is strong and at peace.

Your daughter will flourish as there is more harmony between the two of you. She longs to feel your love and support, *not just your expectations of her.*

I love the honest comments below from girls whose fathers took the time to learn how to better connect with them through participation in The Abba Project. Rest assured that your daughter will say similar things about you if you take the time to do the assignments in this book that are all geared around consistent pursuit of her heart.

Why It Matters to Girls That Dads Pursue Them

"There are more changes than I can say, really. My dad has never really been that keen on talking things out, so the fact that he was not only willing to do this, but stuck with it means the world to me."

"In the past if something was going on, I would usually wait until I could talk to my mom alone. Anymore, though, I just start talking because I feel like my dad and I are closer now so I can talk freely in front of him and with him."

"I know now that he wants to fix or improve our relationship. He's proven that our relationship is very important to him, and he's willing to take time out of his busy, tiring day to work on it. He noticed it was lacking something and went out of his way to make it better. Our relationship became his project."

> "I've gotten a taste of my dad's sweet side, spiritual side, and some of his past. Previous to The Abba Project I didn't always see these things so much. I've learned a lot about my dad in the past year, too many things to list."
>
> "It was encouraging to me as I always wanted my dad to get a better understanding of how I think, see, feel, etc. It was a little hard to respond at first because it did seem a little contrived, but I am starting to see the good in it now—that his intention all along was to learn how to grow in our friendship."
>
> "Even if we have bad memories from the past, now that he has spent time investing in me through The Abba Project, it means a lot to me because he has been trying to reach out to me more."
>
> "I feel that my dad and I have become a lot closer. I am more open with him now about what is going on in my life, including my friends and everything. I don't hide anything now, and it's much better that way."
>
> "My dad has listened more and talked more. He has also been giving affirmation, but also being careful to affirm both the things that are less eternally important (ex: grades) and affirming that things like my heart and my character are more important to him. I really appreciate this."

I'm sure you heard *the heart* in the words of every single girl here. And to support this position, here are the wise words of Dr. Ken Canfield from his book *The Heart of the Father:*

Men Are at Their Best When Their Hearts Are Engaged

> I believe men are at their best when their *hearts* are engaged. The coming generation needs fathers who relate to their children and wives with their *hearts*—hearts that overflow with love and compassion, and hearts that are very intentional and committed to doing what's best for those they love...I believe men possess more power through healthy fathering than in any other area of their lives.

Now it's your turn to clarify the way you are going to intentionally take action *from your heart* in a positive way with your daughter.

I'm going to use my words to pursue my daughter's heart today so she knows I love her by...

CHAPTER 10

AN INVITATION: FROM GOD TO YOU, DAD

I acknowledge that we're not all on the same page when it comes to faith. I state here for the record that my true desire is to be inclusive rather than exclusive.

Inclusive, Not Exclusive

And because I want to model the things I teach, namely the importance of girls being clear and honest about who they are and what they believe, I am choosing to be up front about the fact that I am a Christian who loves God, loves the Bible, loves people of all faiths, and welcomes anyone who does or doesn't hold to the same beliefs as I do.

I truly believe there are enough common denominators when it comes to dads and daughters connecting, regardless of our spiritual beliefs. And **I invite us all to engage in this heart issue together.** I will be sharing things along the way about God and the Bible, and if that offends you or doesn't sit right, please move past those places until you come to the sections that do sit right with you.

Let's All Engage in This Heart Issue Together

My desire is to collaborate and to partner with you at a heart level even if our religious or spiritual beliefs aren't fully aligned.

You heard me tell my story earlier about the origin of The Abba Project. Based on research, not just on the Bible verse about the need to "turn the hearts of the fathers to their children" (Luke 1:17 NLT), I think we can all agree that kids without a dad in the picture are far more needy than kids who have a dialed-in dad. This neediness is also evident in those children whose dad is around physically but not emotionally, such as the dad who responds far more enthusiastically to his team or his job than to his daughter.

Absent Dad = Needy Child

And though we wouldn't necessarily describe a preoccupied dad as contributing to the fatherless dilemma in America, I definitely see parallels between a dad whose heart isn't turned toward his daughter and a dad who simply isn't around. The voids in their daughters are largely the same. My friend and author Dr. John Sowers poignantly says it this way: "The fatherless daughter is on a quest to belong. Her wilting heart guides her choices, wishing to be found again."

We see the heart of God revealed in Malachi 4:6 when He talks about the hearts of fathers *first* turning toward their children, which is *then* followed by the hearts of children turning toward their fathers. There is a sequence here.

Dads must initiate and draw their daughter's heart toward theirs. If a daughter is going to respond, it's because her dad made the first move. It may not happen overnight, but it will happen.

Dads First Must Initiate

Dads have to take the first step in moving toward their daughters. And because God has made girls to be responders (even when there's a "no trespassing" sign on the door of her heart), the reality is that when her heart is engaged, she softens and the wall comes down. (And it is interesting that God didn't mention mothers in this verse; only dads get the directive to take action here.)

I resonate with Emerson Eggerichs, author of *Love and Respect,* who says that respect comes more naturally and easily for men whereas love comes more naturally and easily for women. (Of course men also give love, but Dr. Eggerichs is talking about the ease versus the struggle that tends to exist in men and women in these areas.) This is why God commands men to love their wives and women to respect their husbands (Ephesians 5:33). These God-given commands target the areas of typical struggle for both men and women.

Heart It Is

Further, God doesn't command a woman to engage with her children from her heart (her love center) because the act and art of loving comes naturally to her. But the fact that God talks about a father's heart (not his head) turning toward his kids is most likely because it is less natural for men to stay connected and dialed in at a heart level.

Again, I'm not saying that it doesn't happen, **but the heart connection is something I hear girls say they long for more often with their dads than their moms.** Girls talk about their struggles with feeling (or not feeling) their dad's heart consistently turned toward them, especially as she gets older and begins to develop her own identity. But every daughter really wants and needs her dad.

I continue to be inspired by dads who are willing to invest their time and effort to learn how their daughters are wired. I asked one such dad, Carl, to share his story by writing a letter to other dads.

From One Abba Project Dad to You

Dear Dads,

This journey you are about to embark on will be a very rewarding time of your life, not just for your relationship with your daughter, but also a real probing journey for yourself. You will learn a lot about your daughter and about what makes you tick as a father *and* as a husband. I was fortunate enough to be able to participate in The Abba Project and I can say, without any hesitation, that it was one of the best experiences I've ever had.

To be honest, at first I didn't think I would get much out of it because my relationships with my daughters were good. *But*, this class was a journey, a real eye-opener, a life changer, a time of growth, a time of building deeper and more meaningful relationships, and it led to so many deep discussions. Through The Abba Project I was able to learn to ask probing questions, questions that really meant something.

I grew personally and my relationship with both of my daughters grew exponentially.

And to give a perspective from the other side, here is what Carl's daughter Alexis wants other dads to know about the importance of intentionally pursuing their daughters' hearts.

Through the Eyes of an 18-Year-Old Daughter

The Abba Project totally improved my relationship with my dad. As a dad you have obvious interest in growing closer to your daughter and getting to know her on a different level than only what she lets you see. What you are doing will be the best experience of your life.

My dad decided to participate in The Abba Project because I was in counseling for an issue I had with guys. My dad and I had an okay relationship, but I never felt comfortable opening up to him about my struggle with guys or my self-image.

Over time I came to realize that part of the reason for my guy issue was that I had a "daddy void." My dad hadn't been there in the way I needed him to be when I was little, but through this class we were able to grow closer than I ever thought was possible. We were able to finally talk about the tough stuff.

I learned so much about my dad and found that we have more in common than I ever would have thought. I have come to respect my dad even more than I already did. I wish he could take this class again because I would love to continue to get to know my dad with this kind of focus.

To all the dads out there, I encourage you to go all in and to put your heart on the line for your daughters during this process. Not all of your daughters will respond in the way that you would like them to, but don't let that keep you from reaching out and chasing them with your love. A girl wants to be chased and desired; your daughters are no different.

Chase her and let her know you desire to get to know her for who she is on a personal level. She will appreciate it, even if she doesn't verbalize it to you. Don't give up on her or on yourself.

Chase Her with Your Love

As Alexis said, don't ever stop pursuing your daughter's heart. Instead, *chase her with your love.*

You as a dad have the God-given assignment to

- *engage* your daughter's heart
- by *turning* toward her
- and *inviting* her to do the same

You have to make the first move. She'll come toward you if you are lovingly consistent in your pursuit.

If you're a visual processor, perhaps this picture will make it clearer. Have you ever forgotten to water your plants for just one day in the heat of summer, only to discover that they had wilted and looked like they weren't going to recover? I recently had that happen and couldn't believe how quickly my plants went from life to death merely by a lack of water. But then the miraculous seemingly happened when, with one good watering, they quickly sprang back to life.

Your daughter needs you to pour life into her daily because even one day without your steady love and attention will cause her to wilt. If you turn your head, even for a moment and forget to invest, she will suffer.

She Needs You to Water the Soil of Her Heart

Now it's time to make it personal as you renew your decision to accept God's invitation as a dad with your daughter.

I am going to partner with God to engage my daughter's heart more effectively right now in her life by...

CHAPTER 11

WHAT I'VE DISCOVERED ABOUT MEN...THE LONG VERSION

I know you said you want me to get to the point already. You're ready to get to work, yet here I am using my twenty thousand words a day when you're comfortable with your seven thousand. But I believe this chapter is vitally important because the better you understand yourself, the better leader for your daughter you'll be.

Prep Before Painting

Think of it this way: When you paint a room, if you spend the painstaking time to tape off the baseboards and window moldings first, the job goes much faster and more efficiently. Likewise, if you spend time here on the front end to explore yourself, the whole project will flow with greater ease and efficiency because you will be clearer and more focused.

The following realities impact dad-daughter dynamics (as well as husband-wife dynamics) and will set a foundation as we move forward on this journey. My hope is also that you'll sense that I both understand and value you as a man.

Here are some of my thoughts in random order. I'll start with one I wrote about earlier, but will expand it a bit more here.

Every Man I've Talked to Says This Is Spot On

1. Men would rather do nothing than do it wrong.

I've had dad after dad affirm that this statement is true, regardless of the life arena it may apply to.

Now let's tie it to parenting a daughter. When it comes to relating to your girl, particularly at the onset of puberty, you can probably mark the time when the upsets started happening more regularly. As you well know, most (if not all) of that is due to *hormones.* It is here that most men say to their wives, "I'm making it worse. You're a girl—you go in." And then you back off. What I want and need to say to you is, "No, don't pull back. Move toward her. Engage her emotionally. Your daughter needs *you*."

A Key: Don't React to Her Reaction

Dad, let her know that she is more than her reaction. This is a key piece of information to remember. If you react to her reaction, you'll get nowhere. Then it becomes an eruption as the two of you "get into it." I can assure you that I've got quite a few dents of my own from bonking into my dad. But we got through it and we're friends now. Just know that it does improve as you *both* grow and mature.

I know that it's really hard to go into the eye of a tornado when it's coming toward you. And I realize that what I'm saying may seem counterintuitive. But your daughter needs you to head *into* the storm *with* her. Your male energy, believe it or not, calms her down *if you stay calm*. You can be her steady guide in the intensity of her life if you engage her heart rather than merely give her information that she, frankly, often already knows. By simply being there *with her* you are giving her a gift beyond compare.

You may need to give yourself a time out to calm down first before getting close to her, but then go in. Pray for wisdom (and shielding) and then head in.

This Is Where Good Men Show Their Hearts

Even though some of these tricky relational interactions tend to negatively impact the entirety of family dynamics, *daughters desperately need their dads during their reactive years*, which, contrary to how it may seem presently, won't last forever.

In his book *Bringing Up Girls*, Dr. James Dobson describes what he calls "juvenile puberty" as the time when girls have a high level of estrogen saturation in the brain that significantly impacts their moods (anxiety, anger, irritability, depression, hypersensitivity), behaviors (self-absorption and self-pity, expressed often as selfishness), and thinking patterns (lack of flexibility and obsessive focuses, often on boys, image, reputation, her body).

This occurs two times in a girl's life: between six and thirty months of age, and again during pubescence through adolescence. Entrance into this season and length of time in this season differ for each girl based on genetics. It usually lasts a minimum of five years, according to Dobson. This disequilibrium in a girl's brain impacts her emotional stability (or lack of) as a result of constant rushing levels of progesterone and estrogen, over which she has no control.

She Needs More Attachment, Not Less

Dobson sends a strong message when he asks, "What does a girl need from her parents when everything has gone topsy-turvy? The answer, in a word, is more attachment, not less. Even when she is most unlovable, she needs love and connectedness from her mother, *but also from her father*" (italics mine).

My translation is that you are her lifeline to sanity before, during, and after adolescence.

Be a Lifeline to Her Sanity

It is paramount that you as her dad help her to navigate through these years without giving her negative messages in reaction to her reactions. Get educated on what happens in her brain so you can help explain herself to her. (I recommend *The Female Brain* by Dr. Louann Brizendine and *Bringing Up Girls* by Dr. James Dobson.)

I want to invite you guys to understand a little something about how women view the "doing nothing" response even though this makes sense to you when you choose to avoid failure by backing off. Women translate your inaction as passivity or neglect (which could be true in some cases).

Tell Us What You're Doing When You Back Away

Oftentimes, I believe that a man's lack of action comes from an honest appraisal of his own deficits. It also can come from his desire to defuse an intense situation rather than add fuel to an already existing fire. But please know that we women need for you to tell us (*without getting angry*) what you're doing when you back away because then it helps us understand where you're at without feeling abandoned in our time of need.

2. Men want to keep their women happy.

I continue to be amazed at how men are commonly driven toward harmony in relationships with the women in their lives, sometimes at a cost to themselves. Men will usually do whatever it takes to make their wives and daughters happy. You want to see us smile. This truly is an amazing gift that you men have wired into you. And I don't think that we women tell you often enough how grateful we are that you work so hard to please us. So, on behalf of all women, I say, "*Thank you.*"

But the downside to this is that when your women aren't happy, it's very easy for you to personalize things and believe it's your fault that they're upset. This can lead you to believe that you have to fix it. But when you are emotionally maxed out and she isn't responding to your plan to make it all better, you react from a place of frustration. And by that point usually everyone has moved away from the original goal of connection and harmony, and now everyone is reacting to everyone's reaction.

The Happy-Unhappy Dance

This plays into another reality that impacts the happy-unhappy dance, an interaction that is dependent upon where a man is at with his personal health—mentally, physically, emotionally, and spiritually (because he may not be living from a healthy place in those four areas). Consequently, if his primary goal is to "keep the women happy" without living from a healthy place himself, then he's not giving from a grounded place. This leads to codependence (which is unhealthy) rather than interdependence (which is healthy).

Balance with Boundaries

My suggestion is to choose *balance with boundaries* in taking care of yourself as well as making your girls happy. This involves being able to say *yes* and *no.* When there is attention given to both of these dynamics, you'll have a bigger reservoir to give out of.

3. Men usually feel things deeper than they let on.

You may not appreciate me saying this, but here goes: *Men are more fragile on their underbelly than they may want to admit.*

More times than not I've discovered that men are more sensitive on the inside than what they are willing to reveal on the outside. Yes, by nature men are hunters and gatherers and warriors and champions. Men are wired to fix and do and lift and lead. Men are taught to be tough and strong and bold. But then when something conflicts with these primary drives, men tend to ignore or diminish anything that stands in opposition to their core instincts.

What Tool Do You Use to Offset Emotional Intensity?

When men feel disrespected, belittled, criticized, or rejected, they often will react, push back, or use anger as a way to get the power back. By way of contrast, some men may retreat or isolate as a reaction to these same relationship dynamics if they feel the fight is useless. Then by backing off, they disconnect from the frustration or sense of being overwhelmed in order to cool down.

Many men flood with intensity when they are feeling helpless or incompetent. But rather than connect to these seemingly weak feelings, they often use anger or withdrawal as a coping mechanism. And because men want to stay calm under pressure—at least on the outside—they aren't always aware that their intensity is rising while they help to defuse a crisis by stepping into rescue mode. Then when their max threshold has been reached and limits of patience are abruptly over, their anger blasts out.

Start by Being Honest with Yourself

Begin by being honest with yourself about the emotions that are underneath your anger (fear, sadness, confusion) or underneath your withdrawal (hurt, rejection, helplessness). If you can admit and connect to your primary emotions, you will better navigate your choices, particularly in crisis, and your relationships with the females in your life will be much richer and healthier.

4. Men are often driven by crisis or need.

I've had many dads ask me why I don't have an additional Abba Project group for dads with younger girls. My response to them is this: "Because I find that men aren't usually motivated to add yet another thing onto an already full plate unless there is crisis or need." Then I let that sit for a minute and most every time I have gotten an affirmative response.

What Motivates Men?

Before puberty hits, dads usually find it fairly easy to connect with their daughters. Of course there is the occasional hiccup, but more often than not, before the hormones of adolescence set in, girls are fairly easy to connect with.

But then one day everything changes. Some parents describe it as "a switch that suddenly flips on" (or off, depending how you look at it). The once happy, playful little girl now tends toward being moody, irritable, overly sensitive, less communicative, and for some odd reason, now prefers her friends over you, her parents.

And to make matters worse for you, dad, instead of the days when she was "Daddy's little girl" and you could kiss her boo-boos and make it all better, she now doesn't run as readily to you. Instead, she gives far more credibility to what an equally mercurial prepubescent girl or immature, testosterone-driven boy has to say.

It's at this point in the dad-daughter relationship that dads are often highly motivated to do whatever it takes to connect with their daughters. It's here that men realize they need more effective tools to speak their daughter's language. It's here that men will take the time to meet with me to learn what to do.

The Male "Fix It" Gene

I believe this plays into the male "fix it" gene where the driving philosophy is "If it ain't broke, don't fix it." When your daughter was younger, you may have looked at the lay of her land to see that she was doing great. Back then it became easy to defer to her mom on the more emotionally complex issues.

But when her emotional intensity began to invade your house, you became very motivated to do something. Anything. You heard yourself using your dreaded dad voice as you shouted, "I'm-serious-this-is-not-going-to-be-tolerated-in-my-house-missy." Yet you soon realized that this approach wasn't working because she was still the vulnerable, soft little girl somewhere inside who couldn't understand why you were suddenly so mean. And then she seemed to be even more lost because you once were her ally, but now she feels that you aren't on her side anymore.

Crisis and Need Are Great Motivators

And you? You're standing there completely baffled because none of this makes sense to you. She makes no sense to you. *Where did things go sideways?* you ask yourself. As far as you know, you're the same you. *She's* the one who has changed, or so you tell yourself. That's when I find that men are willing to do anything to connect with their girls. Crisis. Need.

The upside of this was well stated by my Abba Project coleader, Clay: "We are designed to excel in crisis, that's for sure. I love that God gave us that wiring."

The fact that you're the one she calls when her bike is broken or her bedframe comes unhinged or her car runs out of gas or her financial aid is messed up just proves that you are golden in a crisis. It's then that everything suddenly becomes clear for you and you rise to the occasion. I realize that you don't do well when the crisis doesn't resolve itself, but when your girl needs you, her dad, you're there. Again, this is where you men shine, and I want to thank you.

5. Men hold information in the vault.

One thing I deeply appreciate about men is that information pretty much stays in the vault. As a general rule, men don't spill the beans. Even when their wives or daughters try to pry something out of them, men are typically close-lipped, particularly when it involves protecting a close relationship. That's the upside of the vault.

Keeping It in the Vault

The downside, however, is that the same vault that protects and serves as a positive resource can also turn into a place that holds secrets (pain, failures, addictions, struggles), hidden even from the man himself.

And this is also a challenging problem for men when they don't remember to tell their wives and daughters certain things. And then women feel hurt and interpret this as saying they're not important enough to be told certain things. At times like this you're in a different part of your brain, and you're not meaning to cause intentional harm or distress (as I discussed under point 2).

On the flip side, if women can see the positive part of this—that men aren't going to tell other people their secrets or private details—it can be seen for the strength that it is.

6. Men are prone to go it alone.

This one may seem to be an incorrect observation due to the way married men, for example, tend to be lost when their wives are gone for any length of time. Or the fact that divorced men remarry faster than divorced women. It could seem that men thrive only when their girls are around.

But I am speaking more to the dynamics of men struggling to open up and connect emotionally with other men. Maybe it's tied to the belief among many of them that it's wimpy to talk about feelings or needs or struggles or failures with other men. Regardless of the reason, an underlying driving force seems to keep men from opening up about the hard stuff.

Opening Up Is Hard to Do

More often than not, men hold things in and don't talk about what's really going on inside (granted, this is a generalization and doesn't necessarily apply to all men). I've also noticed that men are not inclined to ask for help, such as asking for directions, even if they really could use it.

Yet for you to become a dialed-in dad, this is one area that has to be conquered. This is where the group format is helpful because it allows men to come alongside other men. This is one of my favorite parts of The Abba Project. When one man risks vulnerability, others follow. A dads' group enables men to walk with one another through the encouraging and the discouraging times with their daughters. I truly believe that men need safe places to unload, and if they don't find this release in supportive relationships, they will tend to disengage from people and pour their energy into their jobs, hobbies, sports, and exercise, just to name a few.

Risking Vulnerability

I have seen positive growth in dads as they have connected in this way with their own hearts through investing in a deeper kind of relating with their daughters.

7. Men often think that listening is lame.

Okay, the way I said this may be a little dramatic, but I was looking for a word that highlighted the fact that the act of listening doesn't seem to be enough to most men. It just isn't cool or macho or manly to "just sit there." I think it taps into the need-to-fix-it part of male DNA where "just sitting there" feels like you're doing nothing.

But in our world as girls, *when you listen, and actually listen to understand (not just give advice), you give us the best gift ever!* Trust me on this one. By being there to listen to your daughter, you will calm her down and diffuse her intensity. Your presence is enough...honest. (I'll have more to say in chapter 14 about the importance of being an active listener.)

Listening to Understand Is the Best Gift

How am I doing so far? If I'm off base, don't hesitate to challenge, add to, or disagree with me. This is interactive learning.

Rest assured that my true desire is to facilitate greater understanding so that you can have deeper dialogue with your daughter (and even with your wife). Now here's your opportunity to dig deep by asking yourself these two questions:

One area of strength I see in myself based on Michelle's observation of men is...

One area where I need work is...

CHAPTER 12

MY DAD AND I: A PERSONAL STORY

My Dad Learned on the Job

My dad and I dearly love each other, but we've also clashed on and off throughout the years because we're both hardheaded. Neither of us likes to back down very easily. Yet despite the bumps and bruises along the way, I've never questioned his love for me. I respect him as a dad, especially when I reflect on the fact that he had absolutely no model to work from. So if my dad could learn to be a dialed-in dad, anyone can. Here's his backstory.

My dad grew up on the South Side of Chicago as the fourth of seven children, six boys and one girl. There were three different last names among them. Being a devout Catholic family, the kids all attended parochial school (paid for by the church), which provided a structure that was vitally important to their mother. The church helped to feed and clothe their family for most of their life.

Because of the family's extreme poverty, my dad learned to work from the time he was six years old, helping his older brothers with their paper routes. At age nine he persuaded a friend's dad to help him build his own shoeshine box, then headed a couple of blocks away to Vincennes Avenue where he snuck into bars to shine shoes until he was spotted and kicked out. This dauntless work ethic and fearless determination set in motion some incredible relational skills and courageous strength that he drew upon years later when he sold cookware and life insurance as a door-to-door salesman in San Francisco.

My dad's father was an alcoholic and abandoned the family when my dad was only seven or eight years old. Survival in south Chicago meant joining a gang, so my dad joined the Daredevils when he was just eleven years old. He didn't get out until he was sixteen. My dad still has scars on his body that mark that time in his life.

He also spent the summers during high school living and working at a ranch where he did everything from cleaning stalls to bull riding in rodeos, all as a way to make money. He did interface with some good men during those years, which was obviously something he had a dire need for.

It's a Challenge When There Are No Male Role Models

My dad joined the military at age eighteen and was even accepted for admission to West Point but turned it down. He says this was one of those life decisions that might have gone a different way had he been given some guidance and counsel.

Stability was something my dad never knew growing up. With three different fathers among the kids, his older brothers each leaving home around the age of sixteen, with poverty powerfully impacting their family, and with little relational or emotional deposits into his life, my dad had absolutely no idea how to be a father.

After finishing army basic training, my dad was stationed at the Presidio in San Francisco. It was here that he met and later married my mom, a farmer's daughter from Minnesota. Her background was very different from my dad's, but was similarly lacking in healthy emotional connections.

A Blank Slate When It Came to Healthy Parenting

Thus, their combination of little to no healthy parenting models led to a blank slate when it came to knowing how to parent me, their firstborn, when I landed on the scene only five and a half months after they were married. In typical fashion for a dysfunctional family, huge family secrets, unmet emotional needs, chaos, and instability were the norm. And no one ever talked about any of this out loud. Instead, pretending that things were fine was supported, enhanced, and modeled.

My mom and dad became Christians when I was five years old. Things changed dramatically around the Watson home after that. Dad gave up drinking, smoking, and gambling. Mom got involved in serving roles as church started being a weekly event. Life as we knew it was never the same.

Hunger to Learn Is a Valiant Quality in a Dad

Though my dad really had no clue how to be a dialed-in dad, between 1960 and 1974 he became a father to four girls. And even though he lacked a role model, I am deeply grateful that he intuitively understood the importance of playing with us girls. This part came natural to him. I have fun memories of:

- fishing with my dad on the San Francisco pier
- going to parks where he'd hide pennies in the bark dust and give hints about where they were until we found them
- my dad building scooters out of wooden crates and roller-skate wheels

- him writing poems and notes, often leaving them out for us to read on mornings when he left for work or on trips
- being tucked into bed while my dad made up unique, creative, engaging bedtime stories accompanied with a ritual where he would close his eyes and let us "put his thinking cap on" until he came up with just the right story

My Dad Started Being a More Dialed-in Dad by Following Examples from Others

All of this was good. But when it came to knowing how to invest in deeper emotional and spiritual ways, he was lost. So my dad began to go to seminars and followed whatever they said to do. One man said that a good father needed to lead spiritually. So he came home and announced, "We're now having family devotions every morning before school, and we're all getting up fifteen minutes earlier." So we did. And he made it fun.

He went to another seminar and they said it was important to have regular individual meetings with your kids to invest in their lives. I was thirteen years old at the time. He said, "Girls, we're going to start having dad-daughter times, each of you individually with me every other week. I'm going to teach you things about life, and it can be a time where you also ask me questions. The most important thing is that we are spending time together." So we did.

He also took me on my first date at age sixteen. I had to wait until I was sixteen to date, and every guy who asked me out had to meet my dad a few days before our date in order to have a one-on-one talk with him. It was *so* hard to accept this rule because I assumed that no guy would go through those hoops to date me. But I had no option but to do it Dad's way. I now am grateful for his covering over me when it came to how guys treated me on our dates. I was always respected.

For our first official dad-daughter date, we went to the Rheinlander in Portland. (This German restaurant has the *best* cheese fondue. It's a must-see if you come to visit.) My dad made sure that I waited for him to open my car door and to let him pull out my chair for me. I remember it being a bit awkward, but he set the bar high for me to expect similar treatment from the guys I dated.

Perfume Day...One of the Best Days of the Year

In the late eighties, my dad started a Christmas tradition where he takes us girls to Nordstrom to buy whatever perfume we want (he's there the whole time, smelling and helping with the final selection). This tradition is a highlight of my year. And my dad enjoys it as much as I do, which is a *key* to it being fun for me. I think "Perfume Day" needs to become a Christmas tradition across America for dads and daughters. In fact, I know many dads who have started doing this with their single *and* married daughters, and I keep hearing great feedback, especially from the daughters!

I trust you're seeing here that it's never too late to start investing proactively in your girls. My dad had no clue what to do when we were young, but he changed the course of our family's history by responding to what others gave as directives. And you can too.

Your Daughter Needs You at Every Age and Stage

The bottom line is that your daughters need you no matter what age they are.

And whether you had a solid male role model or not, take it from my dad that even without that piece, you can turn things around with your children. My wish and prayer is that you'll glean ideas from these pages that will make a difference in your life and your daughter's life.

Summing up, here are the things I've taken from my dad's story:

Lessons from My Dad to Other Dads

- It's never too late to start "kicking it up a notch" with your daughters—begin right where you are.
- Whether or not you had a positive father role model, you can start today being a strong father who intentionally leads your girls well.
- Your daughters will look forward to their individual times with you, and part of the interaction needs to include talking about things that are on her heart.
- Spoil her from time to time and surprise her in extra special ways that put value on her (such as "Perfume Day").
- Create traditions just between the two of you.
- Pursue her consistently throughout her life. She has only one dad and no one can ever replace you.

Opening the Closet Door of Your Life

I started a fun tradition with my dad a couple of years ago. On the way home from our weekly grocery shopping trips (some dad-daughter dates don't have to cost much), I ask him to "open the closet door." I invite him to tell me a story from his childhood that he's never told me before. I've found that dads don't typically think to tell a lot of the details of their lives to their kids, and I'm here to tell you that we *love* your stories. I can hardly wait to hear about my dad's childhood each week, and I've been writing them all down because they are treasures to me that I don't ever want to forget.

Thanks, Dad, for trusting me with your life stories. I love learning about your life and what makes you, you.

CHAPTER 13

RELATIONSHIP, THEN RULES

I've heard it said that rules without relationship equals rebellion.

The Relationship Formula

So if you, dad, are "the heavy" at home, the one who lays down the law and sets the rules without there being a significant relational deposit between you and your daughter, I can assure you that rebellion is what you're getting now or will get down the road.

The reason? Girls need a lot of relational connection to be able to embrace rules with an open and responsive heart. Relationship first; *then rules.*

The Love Bank

Seattle psychologist Dr. John Gottman has done extensive research on what it takes to make relationships work. I love his concept of the Love Bank. He says that similar to a bank account where there has to be more deposits than withdrawals to keep it from being overdrawn, in a *relationship account* there also has to be more deposits than withdrawals to make a relationship thrive.

According to Gottman, the perfect balance if you want to keep a relational account from being overdrawn is five deposits to one withdrawal. So if things have been rocky between you and your daughter lately, start depositing more than you're withdrawing from the relationship. It's just that simple. And it's just that hard.

We girls hate to disappoint our dads. And sometimes when we feel as if we're one big disappointment to you, our reflexive response is to distance ourselves because we can't stand that yucky feeling in the pit of our stomach. And because disappointing you feels like a *withdrawal* from the relationship account, we withdraw physically and emotionally as a way to guard against an overdraft. That's how we self-protect.

But here's what we girls want to say to you dads:

Please Tell Us You're Happy with Us

"Please tell us you're proud of us, not just because of what we're doing, but because of who we are. We need to hear that you're happy to have us as your daughter. This is a deposit into the dad-daughter relationship account."

I know that men are wired to fix and help and do. You often want to see immediate results from your efforts. However, this process isn't a quick fix. Your daughter needs to see that you are committed to her *over the long haul* without giving up, even if she doesn't respond exactly the way you'd like her to respond within the time frame you've set for her. Show her you are serious about pursuing her heart day in and day out. No rush. Full commitment.

Often when I read a book I get overwhelmed with all the information, even when it's excellent and inspirational. Perhaps that's how you feel about this book about now! I get that. Therefore, to combat *information overload,* I encourage you to go back through what you've read so far and grab a couple of nuggets to take with you. You can make this information your own by freeze-framing the things that click for you.

One thing I need to work on to strengthen my relationship with my daughter is...

It's Time to Fill the Toolbox

As a practical way to bring the relationship-strengthening resources to life, I'd like you to envision holding a toolbox in your hand. Over the next several chapters, I'll be giving you fifteen practical tools to fill that box, tools you can use each day to build or rebuild your relationship with your daughter. *These tools are the crux of what a daughter really wants from her dad.* I guarantee that if you commit to the goal of using one of these tools every day, your daughter will feel you pursuing her heart, and you'll see a difference in her, in yourself, and in the relationship.

PART TWO

Tools for Your Toolbox

CHAPTER 14

TOOL 1: BE AN ACTIVE LISTENER

I'm sure you've heard it said that God created us with two ears and one mouth for a very good reason: He wants us to listen twice as much as we talk. (At least this is one theory!)

I imagine that you might enjoy using these words to encourage your daughter to close her mouth a bit more often. But remember that this is a book for *you,* dad, not your daughter.

As you ponder this hearing-to-speaking ratio, here's a question for you: "*What kind of listener are you?*"

What Kind of Listener Are You?

- a *passive* listener (show disinterest or boredom)
- an *active* listener (engaged, eye contact, lean forward, nod)
- a *distracted* listener (do something else simultaneously, half-listening)
- a *reflective* listener (ask questions, make comments)
- an *irritated* listener (interrupt, push her to end sooner than she's ready, express anger at her excess verbiage)
- a *supportive* listener (aware there's a deeper dynamic here than just the words, ready to help her figure things out by teaching her *how to think, not just what to think*)

Being an active, reflective, and supportive listener takes energy, effort, and intention. It's hard work. And when it comes to your daughter, it's vital to remember that on Venus we girls figure things out by *talking.* (This is true even for introverts.)

We Girls Figure Things Out by Talking

This translates simply to this: we Venusians need a *listener.* And it would be great if the person in the sound booth was you, dad.

As a listener you have a strategic role because if she *has* to talk in order to process, then better it be you than only her female peers or boys who may have another agenda behind their listening.

I Know This Is Hard Work

Okay, I do understand that active listening is harder than it looks. But I honestly believe that **when you are motivated out of love for your daughter, you will and can do anything.** If she sees you as a dialed-in listener, equipped with full attention and without criticism, she will feel your support and open up more to you.

John, an Abba Project Dad, profoundly expresses the way he is learning to make sense of listening to his daughter: "The longer I listen, the more I realize the question I was going to answer wasn't even the question she was going to ask."

Here's a funny thing about active listening: It involves more than just your ears. I realize this may be new information, but it's true. Active, engaged, supportive listening also involves your mouth. But you have to talk *with* her, not *at* her.

Here's How to Proactively Listen to Your Daughter:

- Make eye contact, lean forward, nod, ask questions.
- Be aware of body language and tone of voice.
- Treat her the way you want to be treated—model respect.
- Remove distractions (or set a time to connect later if need be).

Just ten minutes of your undivided attention is better than sixty minutes of your divided attention.

It may even help to think about this from another vantage point: your stance at work. *Would you ever be successful at your job if you turned on the television at the same time you tried to close a business deal?* Of course not. When you're clear about your purpose and agenda at work, you stay focused and can effectively execute a plan of action.

Give Her the Gift of Your Presence

Similarly with your daughter, if you're clear about your heart goal and understand that when you actively listen you affirm her and put value on her, you'll be willing to sacrifice in order to give her the gift of your time and your presence.

It was a joy for me to watch Rick, through The Abba Project, build even stronger relationships with all three of his daughters. Here's how he describes what he learned about listening:

The session on listening has proven to be the one I most frequently put to effective use. Throughout the program, you stressed general differences between men and women. One of the behavior characteristics you mentioned is that men are generally compelled to fix things. You also discussed the fact that women (girls) sometimes just need someone to listen…without taking action. They need to vent—to let out frustrations, emotions, etc. You emphasized the importance of listening and asking more questions, but not putting our girls or their concerns on a workbench to "fix" them.

On the surface, this concept is simple and obvious. In reality it is not. Sometimes girls want a sympathetic ear and sometimes they want Dad to fix it. Knowing that I will never master the art of discerning a "just listen" session from a "fix it" session, I have taken the measure of asking my daughters what session we are in. My oldest daughter (age 24) is fiercely independent. Recently, she called me and began to express her exasperation with her boyfriend. When she got to a pause in her monologue, I asked her if she just wanted to talk or if she wanted advice. She chuckled and told me that, "at this point, I just need you to listen, but later I might want your advice."

I've used this on all three of my girls and learned that they appreciate the transparency of the question. By getting this question asked and answered early in the discussion, most of the uncertainty with regard to the purpose and goals of the discussion is removed, and we can both focus on the true purpose.

What Rick Learned About Listening

Strategizing in Light of Your Wiring and Schedule

Because you know how you're wired and what kind of margin you need in order to engage with your ears, you can strategize accordingly. (This all applies to the way you interact with your wife as well.)

- If you're an introvert who refuels from being alone, you may need to create space (down time) between work and home so that when you walk in the door, your energy is directed toward your daughter rather than away from her.
- If you're an extrovert who is high energy, with a daughter who will open up only if you're mellow, then you also may need to create space between work and home to burn off excess energy (through exercise, prayer, meditation) so you're able to truly listen and pace with her.

- If you relate at home as you do at work and your daughter feels like a client to you rather than a family member, then you may need to intentionally focus on what you want your exchange to look like when you see her. Write down some questions to ask her so that you are poised to hear her thoughts, fears, feelings, opinions, et cetera (aka her heart).
- If you have a schedule that affords you very little time together when she's home, it may help to text more and set up regularly scheduled dates where you both can catch up.

By now you know the drill. In order to make this personal and practical, I invite you to choose your answer (or provide your own) to the following questions:

Where and when it's hardest for me to give my daughter the gift of active listening is...

- ☐ right after work
- ☐ during the game
- ☐ at the dinner table
- ☐ after 10 p.m.
- ☐ or...

My proactive strategy for combatting this dilemma is to...

- ☐ drive around before coming home so there's more margin to listen when I get there
- ☐ set up an appointment to talk a little later in the day and keep that promise
- ☐ make time for one-on-one dates to build a foundation of talking and listening
- ☐ or...

CHAPTER 15

TOOL 2: "I'M WONDERING..."

As I've said, I want to give you pragmatic, well-tested ideas so you can hit it out of the ballpark as a dialed-in dad. This next tool for your toolbox will help make you a more skilled communicator. *I guarantee it will be one of your most used and favorite tools!*

This Is Going to Be One of Your Favorite Tools

I call this the "I'm Wondering" tool. It's a super-easy technique that I've taught to many dads, and they consistently report back that it's their number one help in communicating with their daughters.

All you need to activate this tool are two words: *I'm wondering.*

Here's how it works: When you ask your daughter a question, put the words, "I'm wondering" in front of that question.

It Will Be Heard as a Question Rather than a Command

The addition of these two simple words will *soften your tone of voice,* and your daughter will hear you *asking her a question* rather than giving a command, and she'll be more likely to respond.

I know that we girls are complicated and complex, but if you talk to us with kindness and a gentle tone, we're usually able to calm down and respectfully engage in dialogue. If you don't believe me, just give this a try. I'd love to hear your stories.

We heard from Andy at the beginning of our journey together, and I'm going to let him repeat his story here as a way to illustrate the effectiveness of this tool with a real dad and daughter.

Andy's Story of Success

> I have four sons, and Meghan is my seventeen-year-old wild child. When I started The Abba Project, I had no idea what to do to relate better to her and was desperate for help. Truth is, I'm used to boys, and she was giving me a run for my money.

When Michelle taught us to add the words "I'm wondering" in front of a question, I figured I didn't have anything to lose since Meghan didn't usually respond to my questions anyway. She would usually put walls up and not say anything or her claws would come out and she'd push back.

The first day after learning about this I went home and tried it. I was shocked to see how it worked.

I used to say, "Why aren't you going to school today?" But this time I said, "I'm wondering...why aren't you going to school today?" And miraculously she started talking. I couldn't believe that it worked.

Did you notice that Andy used the exact same words he'd been using, but by simply adding "I'm wondering" to the front of his question, it changed his tone and his daughter immediately responded?

Here's why this works.

Oftentimes as men you think you're talking in a gentle tone to your daughters, but to them it sounds like a harsh command. They hear your words as an order being barked at them. I know you don't hear it that way, and you're confused because your sons never seem to have a problem when you talk to them like this.

Works Like a Charm

But if you want to build a bridge toward your daughter, you'll be willing to put this simple technique into practice. And you'll see that it works like a charm every time!

CHAPTER 16

TOOL 3: QUESTION TO LEARN

This "Question to Learn" active listening technique is one that also works wonders.

A few years ago I heard an author give an insightful and creative lecture on her book, *Learning to Question, Questioning to Learn.* I remember being intrigued as she put images on the screen from a book called *Animalia*, where the pictures on each page corresponded to a letter of the alphabet.

Learning to Question, Questioning to Learn

Then she had us divide into small groups and instructed us to only *ask questions* about items on each page with *no additional dialogue*. For example, some of the questions we asked for the letter *A*, silly as they may have seemed for doctoral students, were: How many teeth does the alligator have? What might be the reason for the armadillo to be backing away from the alligator? Did the asp think he could sit on the ant and not squish the poor little thing? And on it went as question after question was posed.

The point of this exercise was not about asking eloquent questions. *The point was simply to ask questions.*

The Point Is to Ask Questions

I know we've all heard there's no such thing as a stupid question. But in this case we really did ask stupid, even nonsensical questions. Yet it was deeply impacting because we learned to look differently at the seemingly obvious (let's hear it for academia!).

When applied to your relationship with your daughter, this concept places the emphasis on seeking to know what she's thinking by drawing her out with questions. **It's about asking and listening rather than talking and telling.**

Active Listening = Asking Great Questions

Typically, girls like to talk while dads listen. Sometimes, though, dads have stopped listening long before their daughters are done talking. Sound familiar? Part of what will keep you engaged as an active listener is to ask questions that keep you dialed in, a dynamic that invites the question: *How do you ask good questions to help you stay connected while your daughter talks?*

In one of my first counseling courses at Lewis and Clark College, Dr. Joan McIlroy said that the better questions a therapist asks, the better that therapist will be. Similarly, the better questions that you as a father ask, the more your daughter will open up and reveal her heart to you.

A Formula for Active Listening

Here's a simple solution for asking good questions to keep a conversation with your daughter moving: *Take one or two words from something she's just said and use them to ask a follow-up question.* Here's an example of what I mean:

Start with a general question: *"How was your day at school?"*

She answers, *"Fine."*

(Often this is where the conversation ends for most men, but this tool will keep the conversation positively going forward.)

Then ask her, *"What about your day was fine?"*

She answers, *"Well, this really hot guy smiled at me in math."*

You can then ask, *"What about him is hot?"*

I can imagine that she will be laughing hysterically at this point while being too embarrassed to continue because suddenly she realizes that you're not the one she usually talks to about these kinds of things. Yet what you'll see through this process is something akin to watching a flower bloom as the questions peel back the layers of her thoughts and feelings.

Listening Goes a Long Way

She'll keep opening up as you ask each follow-up question. She'll know that you're really listening because you're using her own words to respond back to her.

The best part is that you don't have to come up with a completely different question to let her know you're tracking with her. Instead, you only need to ask her to clarify one or two of her previously spoken words. It's actually quite easy.

I've had many Abba Project Dads find success using this technique to enhance their communication skills with their daughters.

And in preparation for your next dialogue with her, fill in the box below so you'll already be one step ahead. Then have fun listening while you learn to question and question to learn.

My daughter's favorite topics are...

1.

2.

3.

Today I will actively listen by asking her to tell me more about each of these three subjects.

Signed ______________________________

(your name)

CHAPTER 17

TOOL 4: HELP HER FIND HER OWN VOICE

I've heard it said that communication is 7 percent words, 38 percent tone of voice, and 55 percent body language.

If you do the math, you'll see that this means that 93 percent of communication is nonverbal. How's that for significant? This little statistic serves as a reminder that as a reflective listener, *we say more by what never comes out of our mouth.*

More Is Said by What Never Comes Out of Our Mouth

Think back to a time when your daughter tried to tell you something when you weren't fully dialed in, and she then reacted in a way that seemed entirely inappropriate to the situation. And there you were, completely dumbfounded because you had no idea how she leapt from a zero to ten in intensity over something seemingly insignificant. At least to you. Two words: *nonverbal communication.*

In his book *Dads and Daughters,* Joe Kelly talks about the importance of a dad tuning in to his daughter's voice:

A Girl's Voice Is the Most Valuable and Most Threatened Resource She Has

> Girls tend to be a riddle to fathers. Like any mystery, the relationship with our daughter can be frightening, exciting, entertaining, baffling, enlightening, or leave us completely in the dark; sometimes all at once. If we want to unravel this mystery, we have to pay attention and listen, even in the most ordinary moments.
>
> Why? Because a girl's voice may be the most valuable and most threatened resource she has. Her voice is the conduit for her heart, brains, and spirit. When she speaks bold and clearly—literally and metaphorically—she is much safer and surer. Dads must help nurture these qualities.

It's your male, testosterone-packed energy in response to her female, estrogen-coated responses and reactions that lays the foundation to impact all relationships she has and ever will have outside the home.

When you listen to her you are saying, *"You, my dear, are worth listening to."*

When You Listen, She Feels Worthy

Most dads I've talked with tell me they want their daughters to grow up to be confident, empowered, emotionally healthy women who are strong in their morals, convictions, and beliefs. But sometimes these are the same dads who want their daughters to obey without question, compliantly follow their rules, stop any and all intense emotion, and not use their voices to assert themselves.

If you truly want to assist her in this voice-finding venture, here's something to keep in the forefront of your mind: **You can't tell her that you want her to use her voice out in the world if you aren't willing to let her practice finding it, using it, and honing it at home.**

I realize that it's *hard work* to listen when you have no margin after a long day. It's *hard work* to stay calm when she's wordy or mouthy. It's *hard work* to track with her when her emotional intensity is as unpredictable as the weather. But if you want to raise a daughter who is strong, vibrant, healthy, and confident, then you must gently and respectfully respond and interact as she is learning to use that amazing voice of hers.

Yes, this will take a boatload of strength on your part, especially when you want her to stop wrestling through the tough issues of life, from rules or guidelines to spiritual questions to boundaries. Just keep reminding yourself that if you want her to be strong and bold, you as her dad are setting the foundation for her to be a critical thinker by going through these ups and downs *with* her.

As your daughter matures, she will be all over the map in knowing how to properly use her voice. But like anything in life, the only way to gain expertise is with practice. Let her practice with you.

Car Keys and Testosterone

Think back to when you got your driver's permit somewhere around the age of fifteen. Do you recall times when you stepped on the brake a little too hard or when you drove a little too fast and threw caution to the wind? Or what about that time you accepted the challenge to see who could hit 100 mph the fastest?

Whether you knew it or not, there was a lot going on hormonally that impacted your driving. Your testosterone levels were at an all-time high, and your voice (and your entire life actually) was trying to find which octave to settle down in. Attention, memory, spatial ability, and aggression are all affected by testosterone levels. Your body was adjusting and learning how to stay in balance at the exact same time that you were being trusted to navigate a moving vehicle. Kind of scary when you think back on it now, huh?

Yet it was all part of the learning curve. You learned by practice and experience, by doing things too much or not enough.

It's a Process to Find and Use Her Voice

It's the same with your daughter when it comes to finding and using her voice. As she hits puberty (and for many girls puberty is starting earlier so this may apply to your daughter even before the age of twelve), she will use her voice too much at times and not enough at others. She will inadvertently run into walls sometimes, and even crash and burn.

But just like when you were a new driver and needed support as you navigated life behind the wheel, your daughter needs your support as she develops into a young woman who is learning as she goes. Let *grace* be your guide. She desperately needs your *kind encouragement* instead of high expectations, your rules backed by a supportive and respectful relationship, with no criticism or harsh critique so she can find her way on her path to growing up.

I share below some responses from girls between the ages of thirteen and thirty to the question, *What is something your dad doesn't understand or know about you? What would it be like if he knew?* As you read, listen to these girls' heart cries to be heard, known, and embraced by their dads.

Daughters Want Dads to Understand

"I don't think he understands that I can handle things by myself sometimes and that I'm not a little girl anymore. I also don't think he understands that I don't like the way that he asks to know things, and doesn't really even listen to me when I talk."

"I care what he thinks and I am not as stoic as I seem. I don't know what it would be like if he knew about it, but it scares me to think about him knowing that I am vulnerable."

"I don't think he understands how I could have sex at such a young age, but also I know that he doesn't know that I have had an STD before. It would be weird if he knew about the STD because that isn't something a father wants for his little girl."

"My dad doesn't know that for about six years I truly believed that he didn't like me. I felt like everything I did annoyed him and irritated him. I thought I didn't live up to his expectations. I would tell my mom this all the time and ask, 'Does Dad hate me?' I wasn't doing it for attention. I internally, 100 percent believed that he didn't like me and didn't want a relationship with me. It hurt so much feeling like my own father didn't like me."

"Something he doesn't know is the pain that I will always have about some things in our family. I've told my mom about it, but I've never told my dad. I know he'd just blow me off and say, 'There's nothing I can do about the past.' He always says that."

"There are a lot of things he doesn't know about me—just because we don't talk that much and aren't that close. I don't share many details of my life with him. But on a bigger scale, I am not sure if he realizes how much his parenting affected me and how much he hurt me."

Dad, do you hear the heart longings in every one of these daughters to be special to her dad? This is a need, not a want.

Emily's Story

My friend Emily is a wife and mother of two boys. While choosing to parent differently than she was raised, she tells of the pain she felt growing up because her dad *"was always too busy for her."* She talks about him being around physically but not emotionally or mentally. He was a pastor and was doing *"God's work,"* and she knew she couldn't compete with that. Emily recalls sheepishly knocking on the door of his office at the age of seven and being afraid that she was a bother to him. His responses usually confirmed her worst fears. Not only has she carried around debilitating fears like an invisible knapsack ever since, but her childhood insecurities have continued to intersect with every relationship throughout her life. She and her dad have come far in repairing their relationship. Emily is working on healing and letting go. She's finding her voice. It's beautiful.

Be a dad today who helps your daughter to find and use her voice.

A topic that causes me to shut down my daughter's voice is...

My plan to support her through her process of becoming a vibrant young woman with her own opinions and beliefs is...

CHAPTER 18

TOOL 5: BUILD HER UP

As a woman who has interacted with girls for over thirty-five years as a counselor, speaker, educator, and mentor, I can attest that *building self-esteem* is nothing new to girls. In fact, on Venus each one of us has extensive experience with stores and media promising us that if we use their products, soak in their potions, wear their clothes, and adopt their philosophy, then our self-esteem will grow and flourish. And we take the bait. We buy in (myself included).

The Constant External-Internal Conflict Drains Us

But I have yet to see any of these promises work because they address only the outside while ignoring or minimizing the inside, the core, the internal. This is the place where women struggle. The constant external-internal conflict depletes and drains us.

When girls are alone with their thoughts, they tend to berate themselves. *I'm too this or too that, too much or not enough.* Add in the comparison game—with peers, siblings, or famous girls on the covers of magazines—and we *always* come up short. I know it's not a surprise to you to hear me say that this is a *way* bigger deal on Venus than it is on Mars.

Because my main goal with this book is to activate and motivate your heart to engage with your daughter's heart, the next tool you need is a building tool: **choose to help build up her self-esteem.**

Counteract the Negative Voice in Her Head

You're a guy, and guys love a challenge, right? The challenge, should you dare to accept it, is to counteract the negative voice in her head as well as the negative voices all around her that aren't always supporting *who* she is.

If self-esteem is something that can be built, and men love to build, then this could be a win-win for you because you can help build your daughter's self-esteem.

Men Love to Build...So Let's Build

If it was possible for a dad to help build or rebuild his daughter's self-esteem after it had been torn down, worn away, or weakened, would you be in? Since you're this far in reading this book, I know your answer is yes.

First, let's review how Webster defines *build*:

1. to construct (especially something complex) by assembling and joining parts or materials
2. to establish, increase, or strengthen
3. to mold, form, or create
4. to engage in the art, practice, or business of building
5. to form or construct a plan, system of thought
6. to increase or develop toward a maximum, as of intensity, tempo, or magnitude

Putting it all together, this means that you have the opportunity in your daughter's life to *increase and strengthen* the core of her self-concept and self-esteem by *affirming* who she is and *celebrating* her uniqueness. You get to help *mold, form, and shape* her identity by consistently *building her up*. As you *construct a plan* to *encourage* her to be her authentic self (even if she chooses a different path than you wish or choose for her) while steadily *increasing the tempo and magnitude* of your positive input as she grows older, you will see that her self-esteem will increase proportionately.

You've probably read that when kids feel good about themselves, there are definite positive results, ranging from higher grades in school to less anxiety and depression to lower rates of teen pregnancy. Clearly, a positive correlation exists between an internal sense of "being okay" and an outward expression of confidence resulting in healthy life choices.

Self-Worth = Self-Esteem

I oftentimes prefer the word *self-worth* to *self-esteem* because of the potential confusion with these two terms. *Esteem of oneself* could be thought of as arrogant self-focus where it's all about me. Yet the word *esteem* means "to regard with respect," "high consideration," or "prize."

These Three Are Worth Every Ounce of Your Investment

Can you see how *esteem* is undergirded with a foundation of worth, respect, honor, and value? With this kind of solid base supporting the relationship between a dad and his daughter, she will have a balanced and positive view of who she is.

When a girl has a healthy self-esteem...

1. She knows that she is worthy of being loved and being treated right. And when she embraces the truth that she is valued, she then makes good decisions about herself and others based on a deep sense of knowing that she merits being treated with respect.

2. She doesn't need someone else to define her, and she can set and express boundaries, opinions, and decisions. She knows how to use her voice, saying yes and no to those around her while being willing to stand up, stand out, and stand alone for things she believes in. She won't be easily intimidated by guys or girls, nor will she bend to peer pressure when her self-esteem is clear.

3. She can hold her own because she is grounded, confident, and happy with who she is. Whether her relationships are with guys or with girls, she doesn't need them to tell her what to think or who to be because she can trust herself. And because these things are worked out in the context of her relationships, it takes a heavy dose of interpersonal learning experiences (which hopefully are positive with you) for her to figure it all out and lock it in.

She Will Internalize Your View of Her

When you approach this issue of self-esteem with your daughter, just remember that *when she knows and feels* that you delight in her, she will internalize your view of her and adopt it as her own. She probably won't even know that her view of herself has anything to do with you, but just between you and me, it most definitely does. You can hold that as your little secret.

So every time you see her succeed, or even learn the hard way by tripping and falling, you can rest assured that her view of herself and the way she holds herself has a whole lot to do with you.

A Forever Deposit: That's Security for the Future

You are making a forever deposit into her heart and life every time you esteem her. Sometimes it will be with your words and sometimes it will simply be the way you look at her. Never stop reminding her that she truly is a prize, your prize, a valued treasure. I promise, she'll never get tired of hearing those words.

Worth, respect, honor, and value. It starts with you. Then it will become her own as she esteems herself with balance and grace.

So let's focus on the nuts and bolts of this building project. It's time for these truths to burrow themselves down into your soul, leading you to take action as a self-esteem builder in your daughter's life.

The area where I tend to tear down (or struggle to build up) my daughter's self-esteem is...

My plan to build up her self-esteem each day this week is...

It's time for your second dad-daughter date. See the appendix for **"Date 2: Dad to Daughter Questions on Self-Esteem."**

CHAPTER 19

TOOL 6: GIVE HER *QUANTITY* TIME

There are never enough hours in a day, are there? I can assure you that my to-do list is *always* longer than my did-it list. And in a world where we have so many time-saving conveniences, isn't it crazy that we're all constantly running behind?

When it comes to the importance of a dad investing in his daughter, there will never be a season in which huge spans of time magically open in your schedule. The only way to have time with your daughter is to make time. And time investment is *vital* to building your daughter's self-esteem.

Quality Time Does Not Replace Quantity Time

A colleague of mine spoke at a singles retreat and asked the 150 attendees to name a regret they carried from their childhood. One answer came up head and shoulders above the rest: *Lack of quality time and relationship with my dad.* There wasn't even a close second.

The Greatest Gift Is Your Time

The greatest gift we can give our kids is the gift of our time. It makes a statement about their value and worth. Kids know that to give time requires sacrifice.

We all invest (monetarily and relationally) in priorities that have value to us. If skiing is important to you, you'll spend lots of money on ski equipment, lift tickets, tire chains, gas, food, lessons, and maybe even hotels and plane tickets. You could easily spend thousands of dollars on skiing if it matters to you. But if you don't like skiing, then not only will you not spend money on all these things, but you may struggle to understand someone who does.

The Cost Is Quantity Time

In order to truly be a dialed-in dad, it's going to cost you more than just energy and money. *It's going to cost you time*—minutes and hours of face-to-face interacting, talking, connecting, laughing, playing, and listening. I don't see this happening enough due to the busyness of men's lives.

The equation is pretty simple: Value = Time + Energy + Money

As a dad you love your daughter. You probably wouldn't be reading this book if you didn't, not to mention all the other things you're involved in for her sake.

Money Where Your Mouth Is

So the question really is: *Are you putting your money where your mouth is?* **If you say you love her, it will cost you time and money, as any good investor knows.** You may recall that Jesus said it this way, "Where your treasure [money] is, there your heart [love] will be also" (Matthew 6:21).

You work hard to provide for your family, and your job often takes the best part of your time, attention, focus, and patience. By the time you get home, you may have very little left to give. You've used up the majority of your words and energy at work. Real life means that some days are more exhausting than others and some days you have less energy to go around. But the key is to ask yourself whether there's a pattern, day after day, night after night, of not dialing in to your daughter.

I understand that you're both busy. But if you don't stay connected throughout her life, particularly during her ever-changing teen and twenty-something years, it will be harder to reengage later on. Your consistent tuning in is essential to her mental, emotional, physical, and spiritual health.

Are You Too Busy?

When I ask young women to describe their relationship with their dads, a common response is: *"My dad is really busy so we don't connect much. But I don't really care because I'm busy too."*

I have to wonder if girls are filling the gap, the void, and their real need for a *dad connection* by spending time with other people and other things in order to deny or dull the reality of her desire for relationship with her dad. It seems that way to me.

When a dad initiates relationship with his daughter, she will usually move things around to spend time with him. The key is that *you* have to pursue her…regularly.

Consistency Is Key

If you're in a season where your daughter is pushing you away, be patient and keep *gently and consistently* initiating connection with her. If she has felt ignored by you or thinks you've made other things a priority over her, she may put up a wall for a period of time (maybe a long time) just to test you and give you a taste of your own medicine. She may not trust your intentions and won't want to open up just to be pushed aside again. She needs to see that you're serious about wanting to connect with her. Building trust will take time.

It's all about making a *decision*. **You have to decide that she's important**. You no doubt already use decision-making skills in your work, and now you have the opportunity to apply those same skills to your relationship with your daughter as you choose to spend more time with her. I know you say your daughter matters to you. But this is all about getting really clear so that your actions speak louder than your words.

Live with Intention

The subsequent question I imagine you're asking is: *How can I find the quantity time to invest in her when she and I both have less and less of it to go around with each passing year?*

Good question. Here are some thoughts about how to make that happen:

Giving and Making Quantity Time Happen

1. Make a decision to invest. Set times to connect one-on-one with her even if you're tired. She doesn't need to know you're exhausted. She'll remember that you spent time with her. Make it happen. No excuses. We all make time for the things in life that really matter.

2. Pursue her heart. I know I keep talking about your heart and her heart. I'm underscoring the vital importance of this kind of connection, as well as it being a key point of God's focus on effective fathering (Malachi 4:6). Using financial terminology, she is a secure investment. Her worth and value are significantly impacted by the investment of the *quantity* of your time and the *quality* of your time. It's not either-or but both-and.

3. Actively build her self-esteem through your time and attention. She will remember your investment forever. Build a solid foundation now that will last the test of time. Remember that action heroes have to take action in order to be a hero.

In the words of Mark Victor Hansen, cofounder of Chicken Soup for the Soul, "Now is the only time there is. Make your now wow, your minutes miracles, and your days pay. Your life will have been magnificently lived and invested, and when you die you will have made a difference."

It's About Time

And in the words of Jesus from the gospel of Matthew, "Store your treasures in heaven, where moths and rust cannot destroy, and thieves do not break in and steal" (6:20 NLT).

Make the most of the time you have with your daughter and pour your heart into hers. As the 1974 classic song "Cat's in the Cradle" so aptly states, one minute it's your child who's saying she wants your time, but you're too busy. Then you blink and she's grown, and now it's you who wants her time. **All you have is today.**

The change I will make *today* to give my daughter quantity time is...

- ☐ initiate a coffee date
- ☐ call her
- ☐ set up a Skype or FaceTime talk
- ☐ take her to lunch
- ☐ or...

CHAPTER 20

TOOL 7: USE A MOUTH GUARD

We've all heard the infamous childhood nursery rhyme: *"Sticks and stones may break my bones, but words will never hurt me."* How insane is that? Of course words hurt. Words can always hurt. As we learned earlier from my young friend Olivia, verbal injuries (heart hurts) hurt far more than physical ones.

Think back to words that were spoken to you as a kid by the bully down the street or by your dad when he was angry, by a coach who saw you mess up, or by the girl who rejected you. You still remember them, don't you?

The Long-Term Impact of Words

Words stick with us long after they're spoken. Words stick with us for years, often decades.

My mom grew up with a very angry father, and she lived most of her life in fear of him. When she was first learning to drive, her dad coached her as they drove on narrow country roads in southwest Minnesota. To this day, in her late seventies, my mom still believes she isn't a good driver. Her dad's voice continues to ring in her head, telling her that she has a "lead foot." Though these words were spoken over fifty years ago, they still hold her hostage today.

This reminds me of our dog, Tasha, a sheltie who was a part of our family for fifteen years. When we first got her from the pound at one year old, they told us her former owners had abused her. And though we gave her a loving home, she was always skittish due to words spoken to her in that first year. *If a dog is this affected by harsh words, humans must be all the more.*

The One Hurt Remembers Longest

Sometimes we're on the receiving end of hurtful words and sometimes we're on the giving end. Sometimes we remember what we've said that hurt someone and sometimes we don't. **The person who remembers the longest is the one who heard the words, not the one who spoke them.**

Time to Make Amends

If you have spoken hurtful words to your daughter, it's imperative that you make amends so she can heal. I guarantee that those messages have been deeply internalized within her and have taken on a life of their own. They need to be cleaned out and talked out. You can begin the process of forgiveness by admitting the hurt you've caused her. Listen to her story with absolutely no defensiveness.

Another way to think about words is in relation to their power.

Power Words and Loaded Language

Power words are words that *influence*; they have *leverage, strength,* and *weight.* They can be positive or negative. They tend to linger with both the speaker and the listener long after they are expressed.

Loaded language carries the same basic meaning as power words, but these words pack a punch with their delivery. The picture that comes to mind is a gun that's cocked and loaded. It could easily go off. Anything or anyone in the pathway of the stray bullet will be struck, wounded, or perhaps even killed. Similar to a literal gun, *loaded language sprays words that pierce the heart and soul while carrying strong emotional overtones or connotations.*

Here are some *positive* power words and loaded language:

love	*happy*	*outstanding*	*inspirational*	*lovable*	*deep*
breathtaking	*enchanting*	*awesome*	*exceptional*	*beautiful*	
remarkable	*extraordinary*	*stunning*	*sweetheart*	*precious*	

Here are some examples of *negative* power words and loaded language:

fat	*ugly*	*needy*	*cow*	*disgusting*	*hate*	*big butt*	*slut*
always	*never*	*baby* (immature)	*overly sensitive*	*brat*			
pig	*disgrace*	expletives or vulgar names					

Maybe you're convicted as you see some of the words you've used. Or maybe you feel relieved because you don't tend to use these types of words. Or maybe your response is similar to what John, an Abba Project Dad, recently said, "The thing I learned was that *always* and *never* are right there by the expletives. I've never thought of it that way. That was my takeaway."

When it comes to the need for congruence between heart and mouth, the New Testament book of James says it best: "With our tongues we bless God our Father; with the same tongues we curse the very men and women he made in his image. Curses and blessings out of the same mouth! My friends, this can't go on" (3:9-10 MSG).

I'll never forget the time in my counseling office when a dad said to me in front of his daughter (who had just been released from an inpatient eating-disorder facility after weighing only eighty-eight pounds when admitted), "She's always been the most needy of all our kids." I was horrified and thought, *If this is what you're saying in front of me, what on earth are you saying behind closed doors?*

Watch What You Say: She'll Never Forget

The following two lists provide some examples of what to say and what not to say. Believe it or not, as with the above illustration, some of these are *word-for-word* statements I've heard in my office. Use these lists to do some self-evaluation of your responses to your daughter.

To Speak or Not to Speak... That Is the Question

What not to say:

- You got yourself into this mess so don't come running to me. You have no one to blame but yourself.
- Stop crying. You're just being a big baby. On top of it all, you're too old for this behavior. It's about time you grew up.
- Do you know how utterly ridiculous you sound right now?
- You are wearing me out. I don't know how much more of you I can take.
- You drive me crazy.
- When are you ever going to start acting your age?
- I'm going to call your friends and tell them that you act this way.
- How on earth do you have any friends?
- Shape up or ship out.
- In my house, you will act the way I tell you to act.
- Do you want a taste of your own medicine?
- Can't you ever think of anyone but yourself?
- God must regret having made you.
- You are a big disappointment to me and a disgrace to this family.
- What did I ever do to deserve having to deal with a daughter like you?

- Why can't you be more like your brother/sister?
- It looks like you've put on a few pounds. We're going to have to change your name to Porky.
- At the rate you're going, no wonder no guys want to date you.
- Why do you always make mountains out of molehills?
- Aren't you the drama queen. I think Broadway is looking for a new actress.

Definitely a Good Idea

What to say:

- What did I do to deserve such an *incredible* daughter like you?
- Do you know how grateful I am to be your dad?
- You look so beautiful today.
- You get prettier with each passing year.
- You're right, I don't understand you right now, but I *want* to understand. Can you help me understand?
- I'll be here for you no matter what—any time, day or night.
- I want you to know how much I enjoy you.
- You are going to make a great wife and mother someday.
- I've seen so much growth in you (list specifics).
- Tell me what you're learning in school (or at work). I'd love to hear.
- What was good about your day today?
- What was hard about your day today?
- God broke the mold when He made you. You're one of a kind.
- You are completely unique and gifted (list specifics).
- I love you just the way you are.
- You could never be a disappointment to me, no matter what you do or don't do, because I love you unconditionally.
- What a treasure you are. Any guy who gets to date you (or eventually marry you) is a very lucky man.
- In my eyes, you're the best of the best.
- I am so proud of you.

- I love you.
- You are amazing.
- No matter what, I will always be your main man.
- When is our next date? I can hardly wait to connect with you.

A Grown Daughter's Heart Cry

In a recent blog by journalist Marlene Molewyk titled "The Immense Value of a Father's Verbal Affirmation," she writes:

> I know my father loves me, but I've rarely seen it in his eyes. Instead, the emotions I usually see when he looks my way are disgust and anger because I've made spiritual, career, and child-rearing choices that reflect who I am, rather than who he wants me to be.
>
> His words have reflected these emotions far too many times, and I've ultimately been forced to forge my way through life without my father's verbal love, encouragement, or acceptance. I've gotten used to living without these things, and over the years, I've learned to lean on my heavenly father's love, encouragement, and acceptance instead.

Dad, especially after hearing Marlene's heartfelt words, I'm hopeful that you will take the challenge and choose *daily* to actively, verbally engage in watering the soil of your daughter's heart.

Reworking the Sticks-and-Stones Theme

And if you really want to go the extra mile, why not rework the sticks-and-stones theme by following the example of valiant Old Testament men who would gather stones to make a monument wherever and whenever God did a miracle (more on this in chapter 43: "Building a Legacy"). In like fashion, go outside and first find some stones. Then write loving words on them to your daughter. Make her a monument of love. She'll treasure it...*forever.*

I make a commitment to God and myself that from this day forward I will guard more closely the words I say to my daughter and commit to *never again* say the word(s)...

And here on the front end of this commitment, I encourage you to make amends where your words haven't been congruent with your goals. Ask for forgiveness so you both can heal. And if your daughter isn't open to talking with you right now, you can always put it in writing.

It's never too late to put current truth into the place where the hurt has been. This will go a long way toward *her* healing. And it will go a long way toward *your* healing.

This leads into part two of this commitment you are making with your mouth to express positive words to your daughter.

I make a commitment to God and myself that from this day forward I will guard more closely the words I say to my daughter and commit to *increase usage* of the word(s)...

Time for date number three. Use this time with your daughter to actively listen to her words while using yours to speak life into her. See the appendix for **"Date 3: Dad to Daughter Questions on Words."**

CHAPTER 21

TOOL 8: LEAD WITH VULNERABILITY

I'm sure you remember speaking three simple words to your daughter when she was a little girl, back when whining seemed to be the best way she knew to express what she wanted. (Wait. She's *still* doing that, right?) And you would look at her adorable, tiny face and say, **"Use your words."** You did this for one reason: *You were shaping her for her future where, if she was to become a robust woman who could navigate, survive, and succeed in the real world, she would need to communicate clearly.*

Your Own Words Back to Bite (or Guide) You

So now your daughter is growing up and slowly mastering the fine art of expressing herself verbally (even if most often she practices with friends rather than you). Maybe you're finding now that the tables are turned and *you're* the one who has to dig deep to use *your* words.

We all know that words tend to come at a higher premium for men than for women, and perhaps in your role as a dad you've:

- *trained yourself* to listen more than talk to your daughter as a way to buffer yourself from the weariness of constant dialogue
- *defaulted* to a position of silence or minimal interaction since you're not able to get a word in edgewise anyway
- *learned* to hide behind sports or (fill in the blank), resulting in your being there in body but not really present

Here is what I want to say from my heart to yours:

More Than Just Words, More Than Just Thoughts

- Your daughter needs your words.
- She needs your heart behind your words.
- She needs to know what you think of her, not just what you think.

These three sentences are key tools to connecting with your daughter. Read them again. Read them out loud.

I recently saw an illustration of a giant mouth that was open as wide as it could go with the tongue sticking straight out. And standing smack dab on top of the tongue was a full-grown man staring into that open abyss. If a picture is worth a thousand words, this one says it all. Sometimes as a dad you may feel like you're about to be swallowed up with the immensity, intensity, and enormity of your daughter's words. And even if her words are trapped inside and she isn't letting them out, you know they're there somewhere close because you can sense when she's ready to blow. About this time you're acutely aware that you need more words in order to navigate and connect with (or help lead) your daughter.

Heart and Head Gotta Align

I assure you that the more you open your mouth and let yourself engage in dialogue with her (gently, not in anger), while being willing to be imperfect in the process, the easier it will become to speak Venusian because your heart will open up in the process. She'll carry the conversation if you keep asking questions that *engage her heart.*

One Monday night this past year my dad and I were on our weekly dad-daughter Costco trip, and I was asking him some questions about the topic of words.

"Your Words Wear Me Out"

In an extremely rare moment of vulnerable self-disclosure, he said, **"To be honest, Michelle, a lot of the time your words wear me out.** I just can't listen to you as much as you want me to because of so many words. Half the time you lose me."

I'm not gonna lie. I was stunned. I didn't know what to say at first. Here I was, fifty-three years old, and he had never before told me this. But I was glad he told me because he was being honest. I love honesty. Even when it's hard, honesty means we're getting somewhere. He really did say it as best he could. So we kept talking about it, on and off, throughout that evening. (Bless his heart for talking about it.)

When my dad dropped me off at my house, he made sure to *use his words* to tell me that he loves who I am and loves all that God has done in and through me. And though I still had to swallow the hard pill of knowing that my verbose tendencies were and are too much for him, I felt like a new level of honesty was opening up between us.

My dad sent me an email the next day. It's the longest email I've ever received from him. And though I never thought I'd be sharing our private dialogue with anyone, with his permission I want to model authenticity here with you.

My Dad's Email to Me

> Dear Michelle,
>
> After our conversation last night I discovered that my sleep didn't go well. It wasn't that when I woke up during the night that I was thinking of our conversation but probably on a subliminal level it was there. I think after all these years I have come to the conclusion that of all of my daughters, you are the most like your father.
>
> I guess the reason we clash a lot is because we are so much alike. I love the fact that you are committed to excellence, that you are a hard worker, that you work hard to be forthright and holy, that you give more than you get, that you are generous to a fault, that you love people, that you love doing things right, etc. I guess I see in you so much of me.
>
> So, the only thing I can conclude is that you are just like me in every way except there is the principle of the laws of the harvest at work in that you always reap more than you sow.
>
> A farmer puts two kernels in the ground and he gets a stalk with three ears of corn and hundreds more kernels and that is how it should be. A farmer would never make it if he only got four kernels back for the two he put in the ground. So you are more like me than I ever was [in areas of intensity and perfectionism, he clarified later to me]. Does that make sense?
>
> The problem is how we actualize that as time goes on and I guess we are in the process of learning that. Why does it take so long to get there? So after saying all that, I just want to let you know that your dad will always work hard at love and acceptance and to let you know how proud I am that you are more of me than I am.
>
> I am blessed to have a daughter like you and will work hard at letting you know that. I know it's a trite cliché to say "let's put the past behind us," but all those issues we've had in the past with tree limbs

"You Are More Like Me Than I Ever Was"

and linoleum and power washing are just things and experiences that are unimportant. But what is important is that we continue to encourage each other on the journey for the glory of God because I know that is your heart as well.

Your dad loves you more than you know. Hugs and kisses to let you know how special you are to me, Dad

Your Vulnerability Invites Us to Do the Same

When I got this email I actually had a huge smile on my face. It was real and open. I wondered why it took over fifty years for this dad and daughter to have a true, yet hard conversation like this.

I speak on behalf of many of your daughters when I say that when you, dad, are vulnerable and honest, it invites us to do the same. We will try not to get defensive, but we need you to model it too.

And so I don't leave you hanging, here is what I wrote back:

My Email Back to My Dad

Oh Dad...Thank you for this sweet note. I know we had a hard conversation, yet a necessary one last night. I really do want to work on things, so it helps for you to give me feedback. I would love you to be able to be honest with me and tell me when things bother you.

I need to know when I've used too many words and you are saturated. It helps me better honor your margins and internal space. And even though I "read people" for a living, I often don't know what you're thinking...and so the more you can be honest with me, the better.

I am always grateful for your help and I treasure the gift you are to me. And when I come back with questions and opinions, it's because I am clarifying and voicing my opinions and I need something in terms of explanation.

I know I am intense and strong, and clearly my responses often seem like I'm attacking you. I honestly never mean to have it move in that direction, but am usually in a stance where I am "holding my own" and not wanting to "walk away from a fight" if there is something that isn't sitting right with me or is confusing or if I want to communicate my viewpoint.

That's an interesting insight about me being more than you in terms of the kernel in the ground, and I can see that. I think you're right. And even though you're saying to put the past behind us, I honestly am always okay pulling those things out of the vault, especially when there has been time to settle down, and to later come back to dialogue and clarify.

If those wounds stay in the vault, I think they fester and can easily come back into view when there's a conflict later on. I much prefer to open the vault, clean it out, and be able to walk through each side so there's resolution.

But again, I'll honor what you're saying and not go there but just want you to know that I am open to that always. :o)

And I think you know this but rest assured that I have never EVER questioned your love for me. I know that you have been a huge bridge to God the Father/Abba Father for me where it has been easy for me to accept His love. Who knows...maybe your intensity has helped me dial right in to the intensity of Abba Father's love for me...and that's a good thing.

Thank you for blessing me today with your words and letting me know again how much you treasure me. I value and treasure you too, Dad. And even though my intensity wears you out, I guess we can keep working together to pace with each other since we're wired so much alike. I want to be a blessing to you too.

Love you much, Michelle

There you have it: some honest dialogue between a dad and his adult daughter who is in her sixth decade of life. Proof that it's never too late to change the dance.

It meant the world to me to have my dad use *more words than usual* to tell me what was on his heart. I think a lot of dads struggle to let their daughters inside their heads and hearts, which can often lead to misunderstanding. I'm not pointing the finger just at you dads, but I am encouraging you to set the pace for what you want to see your daughter do. She will respond to your heart if you model it first. *Lead with vulnerability.*

Take a Risk: Lead with Vulnerability

Before we leave the theme of *words*, there's one more chapter that I trust will be helpful in better understanding your daughter in the communication department.

CHAPTER 22

TOOL 9: PUT IT IN WRITING

You heard me say earlier that females speak approximately twenty thousand words per day while males use about seven thousand. Louann Brizendine, author of *The Female Brain,* clarifies that women have many more "communication events" per day than men. This includes *all* that is communicated, beyond mere words. Women tend to activate nonverbal communication cues through body language, eyebrow raising, and gestures.

Girls Hold On to Words

Women not only *use* more words per day compared to men (I know this is a big shock to all of you men), but women *remember* more words than men. This is how our brains are wired. Stated another way, words have great value to females, whether they are communicated orally or in writing.

In relation to your daughter, these factors underscore the importance of speaking vitalizing words into her life because she holds on to words. The words spoken to her play *over and over and over* in her head, both positive and negative. **As her dad, your words can either suck life out of her or they can breathe life into her. It's your choice.**

Contributing Versus Contaminating

Though I've often said that "a little Dr. Phil (McGraw) goes a long way," I once heard him say something that has stuck with me: *No relationship is neutral. At any given point you are either contributing to or contaminating the relationship.*

In light of this, allow yourself to consider whether your communication with your girl is characterized most by:

- not speaking (which is neutral and therefore falls under the contamination category)
- speaking negatively to her or criticizing her (as a pattern)

- regularly communicating words of life to her (this includes loving correction as well as affirmation)

Your Voice Can Counter All the Other Voices

If you haven't fully realized the value and impact of the words you speak to your daughter, start today by choosing *daily* to speak words of life into her. Her soul and spirit need your truth so she can replay your words as a counterpoint to any negative self-talk or negativity she hears from others (see chapter 18, "Tool 5: Build Her Up").

Be the positive, life-breathing voice in her head.

Be the Life-Breathing Voice in Her Head

One of the greatest gifts you can give your daughter is to affirm her through writing. In a world where written communication is most often casual (texts, emails, tweets), a letter in your own handwriting stands out.

Thirteen-year-old Olivia surprised her Abba Project Dad when she not only kept the letter he wrote her but placed it on top of her desk for her friends to see. As you can imagine, this dad's heart melted when he saw the positive impact his written words had made.

The beauty of putting your thoughts, dreams, love, truth, and feelings for your daughter into written form is that she can read and reread it. She will treasure the things you write to her both now and for years to come. (I know this because I and many other girls save our dad's notes.)

If you're a dad who has already begun this practice, then great. And whether or not you've written letters before, here are a few dad-to-daughter letter-writing ideas to add to your repertoire.

Letter-Writing Ideas

- What was one of the first things you remember about her when she was born and you looked at her for the first time?
- What beauty did you see in her then and what beautiful features do you see in her now? (Girls love hearing about their eyes, smile, and unique features that you see as beautiful.)
- Write about a favorite childhood memory you have of her.
- What strengths do you believe she has, both in terms of skill and in her person (her character, personality).
- Tell her specific reasons you're proud of her.
- Write about what obstacles you have seen her overcome. Emphasize such qualities as courage, resilience, strength, commitment, endurance, power.

- Write about dreams you have for her future, whether in the form of your wishes for her or things you pray about for her. Do this without preaching or lecturing, only encourage.
- Tell her what it means to you to spend time with her.
- Let her know that you will always be there for her, telling her what it means to you to be her dad.
- Include the meaning of her name and let her know how you see her embodying that meaning.

Meaning of Her Name

Did you know that when you reinforce your daughter's identity by highlighting the meaning of her name, you are emphasizing and celebrating her *who* (who she is) and not just her *do* (what she does)? It's one of the most powerful ways to breathe life into her because it ties to the core of who she is. During biblical times the meaning of names was much more significant than it is today. I'd say it's time for a comeback! (Information about the meaning of names is available online at www.name-meanings.com or www.babyhold.com.)

The Life Notebook: My Personal Story

As I mentioned earlier, when I was thirteen years old my dad started meeting bimonthly with me and gave me something he called "The Life Notebook." I still remember painting flowers on the front with bright-pink nail polish just to give it a little flair. My poor dad didn't have a clue how to be a dad to daughters, yet when a mentor suggested that he meet individually with his girls, my dad was committed. I was nervous at first because I knew it would be awkward, just him and me. But it got easier over time. My dad led, and we dove in headfirst.

He covered topics of dating, living with fear (since I struggled big time in that area), sibling relationships, and the meaning of my name. I remember initially being overwhelmed at the enormity of what it would mean to live up to my name when I learned that Michelle means *"who is like God"* or *"godly woman."*

But at the same time it was awesome to me that God and I had a deep personal connection because my name was tied to Him. Here I was, an insecure teenager with a bad complexion and wonky emotions, but I felt tied to a Person much bigger than I was. This helped give me a stronger sense of identity beyond what I could comprehend at the time. Learning the meaning of my name gave me something solid to hold on to.

I encourage you today to use your words wisely. Your daughter will play the words you say over and over in her mind. Give her inspirational messages to replay that are full of *life*.

The life-breathing words I am going to speak to my daughter today are...

It's time for your fourth date with your daughter. After writing your letter, read it out loud to her during your date. See the appendix for **"Date 4: Write a Letter to Your Daughter."**

CHAPTER 23

TOOL 10: MEET HER, MATCH HER

But What If I'm the Talker and She's the Listener?

Being a father to one teenage girl is enough to challenge any dad. So I'm sure you'll all agree with me that Todd, an Abba Project Dad, gets extra kudos for still being upright as he has *two* adolescent daughters under his roof. Then add in his other unique challenge: *he* loves to talk and connect while *his daughters* tend to put the brakes on in that department.

Like Todd, you may like to talk more than your daughter. Maybe you've tried asking questions and engaging, but when things consistently go nowhere, you've given up trying to delve into meaningful conversation.

Why She May Not Be Talking to You

With us females, there isn't usually just one reason why something is what it is. Here are some potential factors that could be contributing to her blocked communication with you:

- *Her stage of development*. During middle school and high school, girls typically talk more to peers and less to parents.
- *She's an introvert* and you're an extrovert, so words come harder for her than for you.
- *A "Cat's in the Cradle" thing.* Back when she wanted to talk, you didn't have time for her. And now that you're ready to talk, she won't open up. It may be unconscious on her part rather than punishment of you, but this could be impacting her lack of responsiveness.
- *She's been hurt by you in the past* so her wall is up. It may take a while for her to open up again and trust you. But if you are consistently patient without demanding that she talk, she will eventually be drawn toward you.
- *She may be better with the written word* than the spoken word. She may need you to start with writing—letters, emails, texts, Facebook and Instagram posts.

Stated simply, when it comes to having honest discussions:

Meet Her, Match Her

Share at a 1 and wait until she meets you at a 1
[on a 1-to-10 scale, this is the lowest level of vulnerability].

Share at a 2, then wait to see if she meets you at a 2. See if she opens up at a 3, and meet her at a 3.

Try to match her tone, her body language, her intensity. It will be work, but when it yields positive results, it's worth it. And if she shuts down when you're only at a 1, and it's hard for you not to take it personally, you must back away, calm down, and not react negatively.

Again, I say: *Don't react to her reaction.*

Beware of Overtalking

This also means that if a crack of light finally opens up with her, make sure you don't *overtalk*. Be careful not to say everything you've wanted to say for a long time, and don't keep talking even if she shuts down midway through the conversation.

I've heard of dads who finally have a captive audience and then corner their daughters with lengthy lectures or "words of wisdom" when their daughters are:

- in the car and can't escape
- in their room and maxed out with homework or "friend drama"
- already having an emotional meltdown

A Little Bit About Her Brain During a Meltdown

It's important for you to know that when she's in the middle of an emotional reaction, she can't absorb any new information. Her emotional midbrain is "fired up," flooding the frontal lobe where she thinks and reasons. *You must give her time to de-escalate so that she can take in what you're saying to her.*

Not that it's ever easy to have a tough discussion with your daughter, but there are ways to help increase the likelihood of a positive interaction.

Practical Tips to Address a Hard-to-Talk-About Subject

1. Choose a *time of day* when she is most alert (each girl is different, so watch for when she's in her best mood, not just when you have time or are in your best mood).
2. Rather than address numerous issues at once, *pick only one or two* to talk about in one sitting.
3. *Be highly aware of your tone*, just as you do when you're at work. Keep your tone *kind* (not mean), *soft* (not harsh), *gentle* (not stern), and *loving* (not judging).
4. *Tell her ahead of time* that you'd like "x" amount of time to talk and ask her when that could happen in the next couple of days. Never spring your time demands on her or there will be an explosion. Tell her that you value her time and schedule.
5. *End the talk with something positive*—a hug, a compliment, talking about something she enjoys, getting a treat together.

Learn to Pace with Her

While he was part of The Abba Project, Todd decided to ask his wife for help so he could better engage his two teenage daughters. "I tried a different approach and purposely kept it light and spur-of-the-moment. It worked much better." **The key was learning to pace with his girls.**

Here are some practical ideas to help you do the same:

- *Watch her body language*. Is she looking at you or turning away? If "visiting hours are over," then try to speak in bite-size pieces over time rather than all at once.
- *Notice what's happening*. Is she starting to smile or engage? If so, this may be a good stopping point because having a positive response is good. Then come back later for "Round Two" if need be.
- *Stop and check in*. "Honey, I know you're upset right now and don't want to talk to me. I'll give you time to cool down, but I want us to talk sooner rather than later. I'll come back in ____ minutes (I suggest 60 to 120 minutes), and we can continue this conversation then. Does that work for you?"

Oreo-Cookie Communication

My final communication tip is called Oreo-cookie communication. Think about an Oreo cookie—two chocolate cookies with crème filling in between. Here's a *deep* question: Have you ever wondered why Nabisco never created cookies with more than two times "the stuff" inside? My theory is because we can handle only so much filling. Similarly with communication, we can ingest only so much of the hard-to-take information in one sitting.

Here's a way to have your words *go down better* when hard discussions need to take place. Think of the top cookie as positive (words of affirmation, encouragement, expressions of love), followed in the middle with the negative or hard-to-take information (confrontation, boundary-setting, sad news, consequences), and end with another positive cookie.

Positive: "Hi, Honey, I just want you to know that I'm proud of you for treating your brother with more kindness lately. I noticed last night that you gave him the last scoop of peanut-butter ice cream."

Negative: "I also noticed tonight after dinner that you made fun of him for eating too much, telling him he was a fatty. Could you see what his face looked like when you said that to him?"

Positive: "I know it's hard to talk about this stuff, and I appreciate you being open to talk this through with me. You showed tremendous growth by talking even though you felt big emotion and wanted to walk away. Thank you." (Then hug her.)

When you follow this positive-negative-positive formula, your communication with your daughter will result in a big win.

CHAPTER 24

TOOL 11: LEARN TO READ HER EYES

We've all heard it said that beauty is in the eye of the beholder, a statement that invites the question for dialed-in dads: *What do you see when you look at your daughter?*

Never forget that your view of your daughter dramatically and significantly affects the way she sees herself. In fact, **your reflection of her is one of the most powerful mirrors she will ever have.**

You Are One of Her Most Powerful Mirrors

We all have unconscious thoughts about other people that lead us to either pursue or distance ourselves relationally from them. When we interact with people who respond positively to us, we tend to *move toward* them. Conversely, when we interface with those who respond negatively to us, we tend to *move away* from them.

When you are with your daughter, you are continually thinking things about her that get communicated whether you are aware of it or not. The absolute truth is that she will pick up on *all* of it.

What Do You Really See When You Look at Her?

Not only will she notice, but she will absorb any negative vibe or thought you might have about her. She will see a critical body scan as you look at her or a raised eyebrow in reaction to something she says or a disappointed look when she blows it. She will feel your disapproval, anger, or irritation with her. And she will internalize it, followed by distancing herself from you.

On the other hand, she will intuitively move toward you the more you give positive, accurate, and even corrective (if it's gentle and loving) feedback about who you see her to be. The way you *see* her will impact the way you talk to her and walk with her.

Realize that your daughter looks to you to see herself in your reflection. She wants to know if you see her as beautiful or flawed...a delight or a nuisance...a joy or a pain...a worthy investment or simply an irritation... as someone who is in process or merely a compilation of mistakes.

If you say nothing, she will interpret your silence as something lacking or absent in her. She will assume that she isn't captivating if you fail to respond to what you see when you look at her. *Silence is deadly.*

Here is your assignment:

Once each day for the next week, set a goal to tell her what you see in her that captivates you. You can do this through the avenues of a face-to-face compliment, phone call, text, or written note that daily highlights one positive thing about her.

(And remember that your wife is a girl too and will thrive as you do the same for her.)

We've all lived long enough to be aware that when we look into someone's eyes, we capture a snapshot of who that person is. Eyes are the most vulnerable part of the body because they expose the reality of what's going on deep inside. Whether happy or sad or angry or confused, our eyes tell the story, revealing the hand that has been dealt to the soul.

Our Eyes Tell the Story

Yes, *eyes truly are the window or the gateway to the soul.* And as hard as some may try to mask that vulnerable window, if we take the time to peer in, the truth of what is going on inside will reveal itself.

If you look into your daughter's eyes with true intent to learn and know, you will see who she really is and what she feels, thinks, and even what she needs. With practice this really can happen.

Do you consistently get close enough to your daughter to look into her eyes and read what she is saying?

Looking at Her, Looking into Her

The focus so far has been on the importance of active and reflective listening, followed with an emphasis on the way your words breathe life into your daughter as you speak truth that is congruent with your heart. Now the emphasis is on the significance of not only looking *at* her, but looking *into* her.

Listen to these words from a twenty-year-old college girl whose story reflects how these dynamics with her dad have impacted her:

> "My dad has always had a problem with listening. I used to ask my mom why he didn't look at me when I would talk to him. I used to cry sometimes because I felt like he didn't really listen to me. Even when I would say 'I love you' to him, he would respond with 'okay' or 'hmm' or something like that. Him not listening has definitely had a big impact on me. I think it is very important to look people in the eyes and give them your attention when they are speaking to you. With my dad, I rarely get that."

Another Personal Story from a Daughter

Jesus says in Matthew 6:22-23 (MSG) that "your eyes are windows into your body. If you open your eyes wide in wonder and belief, your body fills up with light. If you live squinty-eyed in greed and distrust, your body is a dank cellar. If you pull the blinds on your windows, what a dark life you will have!"

As a dad seeking to intentionally impact your daughter's life more than ever before, you have an opportunity to help her body fill up with light by looking into her beautiful eyes and reflecting a stance that affirms her worth.

The Story Behind Her Eyes

As you gaze into her eyes while tuning into the story behind them, you will help open the blinds to the window of her heart. Be a light to her soul by *engaging* her eyes in a meaningful exchange with yours. *Watch* the essence of her true self open wider and soar as you *interact* with her heart by *looking* into her eyes and *affirming* her. (I know this is very "female language." I'm choosing to write in a way that will bring you along on this journey of understanding how we girls are wired).

Dads Benefit Too

I continually get feedback from both dads and daughters about dads seeing into their daughters' lives with greater precision. And the report I hear repeatedly is that when a dad intentionally pursues his daughter's heart, *he also changes for the better.*

In keeping with the goal of becoming the best dialed-in dad you can be, your practical, action-oriented, kick-it-into-high-gear homework for this chapter is going to be more internal and reflective. I want you to notice what happens *in you* as you choose to be purposeful about reflecting back to your daughter what you see when you look at her.

What I have noticed *inside myself* this week as I have purposely reflected to my daughter how I see her is...

The way my intentional interactions with my daughter have positively impacted me are...

It's time for date five, which will allow you to focus on the beauty you see when you look at your daughter. She needs to hear your words about body image. See the appendix for **"Date 5: Dad to Daughter Questions on Seeing Herself and Body Image."**

CHAPTER 25

TOOL 12: BE HER POSITIVE MIRROR

Time for a little Q & A to see how well you know your fairy tales.

Q: Which fairy tale contains the question, "Mirror, mirror on the wall, who's the fairest of them all?" and who asked it?

A: *Snow White* is the fairy tale, and the question was asked of the mirror by Snow White's evil stepmother who was both jealous and threatened by the beauty of her stepdaughter.

Mirror, Mirror on the Wall

Just to refresh your memory, Snow White's stepmother would ask the mirror this same question every single day. Her wish was to have the mirror affirm that she was the most beautiful woman in all the land.

Though in real life women don't consult talking mirrors to answer the question of whether they are beautiful, yet they do "listen" to the way beauty is defined by magazines, television, movies, and other outside sources. These are our twenty-first century mirrors. Beauty that is defined by culture, by externals, leads a girl away from being connected to her authentic self.

Every Day She Asks, "Am I Beautiful?"

The truth is that your daughter is asking the exact same question that Snow White's stepmother asked. Every single day of her life she wonders, *Am I beautiful?* She wants and needs to know the answer to that question. And she will keep asking and looking until someone tells her that she is.

She needs you, dad, to answer her question. If she doesn't hear it from you, she will find another mirror on another wall who will tell her that she is the most beautiful of them all. Sadly, some of these "mirrors" have a hidden agenda and are ready to tell her what she wants to hear in order to get something or take something from her.

By contrast, you as her dad have no other agenda than to let her know that you see her beauty completely and fully. She will never tire of hearing you tell her what beauty you see in her when you look at her.

Every day we all take in sensory information telling us things about who we are and what we're about, as well as what is good or not good about us. This information is constantly swirling around us, and girls are *highly* tuned in to these dynamics. For this reason your daughter desperately needs your input about the good you see in her in order to counterbalance the myriad of messages she hears all around her every single day.

Give Her Specifics

People "mirror" or reflect back to us the truth or untruth (lies) about who we are. And girls are wired in such a way that they *have* to hear *words* about what others see when looking at them. If you forgo telling your daughter what you see when you look at her, she will struggle to see beauty in herself.

The mirror your daughter looks into has everything to do with how she sees herself. And you are a mirror to your daughter...always. The question then becomes: *What kind of mirror are you? What image of herself does she see when she looks at herself in your reflection?*

Girls Are Hungry for Affirmation

Girls are hungry for affirmation and will stop at nothing until their starved souls are fed. Dad, what your daughter really wants from you is to hear specifics about what you see as beautiful in her:

- What about her eyes are breathtaking?
- What about the way she did her makeup today is pretty?
- What about the color she is wearing looks stunning on her?
- What about her personality is creatively expressed in the way she put together her outfit?

Body-Image Statistics

Speaking of what women see when they look in the mirror, here are a few statistics that I think will blow you away:

- Twenty years ago models in the US weighed about 8 percent less than the average female. Today they weigh 23 percent less.
- In 1995, 34 percent of high school girls in the US thought they were overweight. Today, 90 percent of US teens are concerned about body shape.

- In 1995 Western television was introduced in Fiji. At that time only 3 percent of girls reported bulimic behavior. By 1998 that figure jumped to 15 percent, with 74 percent reporting that they felt "too fat."
- The number one wish of girls ages 11 to 17 in the US is to be thinner.
- Nearly two-thirds of teenage girls admit to thinking about improving their body in some way every single day.
- In 2008 *Self* magazine polled 4,023 women, and 75 percent reported disordered eating behaviors or symptoms that were consistent with eating disorders. This translates to three out of four women having an unhealthy relationship with food or their bodies.

If I had a quarter for every time I've heard a girl or a woman tell me that she struggles with looking at herself in the mirror, I would be rich. By contrast, most men don't struggle much with the mirror. This is partly why it's hard for men to really understand this issue for women. Yes, once again we've got a Mars-Venus difference.

Mean Mirrors

I am continually dumbfounded that the girls who tell me they hate what they see in the mirror are the most beautiful and stunning young women. Yet one after another they tell me what messages they hear in their heads when they see their reflection. Here are some typical examples:

You fat pig. You'd better starve today because your body is disgusting.

No wonder guys don't ask you out. It's because you're ugly. Who would ever want to be with you anyway?

Your sister is way more beautiful than you. Bummer to be you.

It's heartbreaking because of the disconnect between the reality of what I see and believe about these women and the reality of what they see and believe about themselves. It's as if we're seeing entirely different people.

I'm Turning You into a Shrink

And just for a moment I'm going to turn you into a "shrink" like me. When you look back at the messages these girls say to themselves (see above), are they in first person ("I"), second person ("you"), or third person ("they")? If you said second, you're right.

And when I repeat back to the girls what I hear them say, and remind them that second person thoughts cannot be their own, they are always shocked. Each girl thinks she's hearing her own thoughts in her head, but they *never* are. It's *always* the voice of someone else. (By "someone else" it could be an internalized voice of someone who has hurt or criticized her or it could be of a spiritual origin. I'll address that more in chapter 30, "Romance and Royalty: The Threat.")

She Needs You to Fight for Her

Can you see why I'm activating your heart and head here? **It's so you can stand up as a warrior and help fight *for* your daughter and *with* your daughter.** This negative voice isn't her own and she needs *you* to do battle for her so she can see herself as she truly is. It's hard for her to always differentiate between her thoughts and these negative *other* thoughts. This is where you can step in.

Here's your practical battle plan:

Every day this week, write *messages on her mirrors* (bathroom, bedroom, rearview or visor mirror in her car) using an erasable marker or sticky notes. Give her *truth* that will enable her to see herself from your vantage point as her dad.

CHAPTER 26

TOOL 13: LIGHT UP WHEN YOU SEE HER

One more way to frame this concept regarding the way you see your daughter comes from a delightfully quirky movie called *Mr. Magorium's Wonder Emporium.* I know it's a chick flick, but it has some really great lessons in it. So here goes.

The story is told of the most strange, whimsical, and marvelous toy store where the toys spring to life on cue. Mr. Magorium has magically infused the shop with the same delightful energy that is innately found in children, an energy that is activated when their curiosity and enthusiasm come alive through play.

Dustin Hoffman plays the role of a 243-year-old eccentric toy store owner named Mr. Magorium who announces he is "leaving" (a euphemistic way of saying he's dying). Yet before his departure, he decides to bequeath his store to an insecure, awkward, and floundering young woman named Molly Mahoney, played by Natalie Portman. Although an accomplished pianist, she lacks any confidence in her musical ability, let alone any possible skill to run the toy store. Mr. Magorium's abrupt declaration that he is leaving sends Molly into a tailspin as she comes face-to-face with her debilitating insecurities.

Needing to Prove She Is More than She Believes

Molly is described as "needing an opportunity to prove that she is more than she believes." Thus, Mr. Magorium creates this opportunity for her to embrace her innate potential, gifting, and strength by announcing that the toy store is hers. He wants her to rise to the occasion and discover what he has seen in her all along. *But instead of pushing through her immobilizing fears, she walks away from the opportunity.* She doesn't believe she has what it takes to succeed. Well, until the end of the movie, that is.

An accountant named Henry, played by Jason Bateman, helps to assess the financial future of the store. He is finally the one who communicates his belief in Molly's ability to bring the store to life by sharing some pseudo-fatherly truth. Henry tells her that if she believes in herself, then the toy store will take on *her* passion, *her* life, *her* energy, *her* joy. But despite his attempts to convince her, she cannot seem to move past her self-doubt.

Girls Long to Know How They Are Seen to a Guy

As Molly wrestles with finding her place in her own life story, she turns to Henry and, with her eyes cast downward, asks him, **"What do you see in me?"**

As a guy, he doesn't really understand what she means, and he tells her so. So she rephrases her question and asks, **"Do I sparkle?"**

Once Henry tells her that she does indeed sparkle, Molly is then able to see it in herself and believe it to be true. Henry's belief in her, his view of her, and his gentle response to her (where he mirrored what she couldn't see in herself), is a turning point for this impressionable young woman. He inspires her to tap into what is already inside her: *strength, passion, creativity, gifting.*

Do You Light Up When You See Her?

"Being the sparkle in someone's eye" is something my dear friend and colleague Dr. Jim Friesen talks about in his book *The Life Model: Living from the Heart Jesus Gave You.* He says that some neurologists describe this concept as our most basic human need: **Not only to be that sparkle but to feel the joy inside when someone lights up upon seeing us.**

Because little children can feel this joy in loving relationships, Jim says that much of life is spent trying to reconnect with that feeling. Life makes so much more sense when people around us reflect back the authentic joy that comes from simply seeing us and being with us. There is healing power in this life-breathing exchange.

Joy Is Relational and Contagious

Jim goes on to say that because joy is *relational*, it is also a *contagious* experience. Joy is produced when someone is "glad to see me," which then stirs up a bit of joy in me. And when my joy is returned, there is an increase in the giver's joy as well. It's a reciprocal dynamic.

This experience, in fact, goes back and forth at amazingly fast rates—six cycles per second in a nonverbal, face-to-face exchange—all the time creating a stronger joy interaction between both people.

So what does this mean for you as a dad with your daughter? Here are some important things for you to know:

What She Needs from You

- She is innately wired with the need to be the sparkle in someone's eyes.
- If not yours, she will be drawn to someone, anyone who will light up upon seeing her.
- Your visual delight upon seeing her will deposit worth and value into the core of her being.
- If you actively reflect back to her the joy you feel when you look into her eyes, it will build her self-esteem as a gift from you to her.

Every Girl Needs to See Her Dad's Eyes Light Up When He Sees Her

I believe that every girl needs to be the sparkle (or the light) in her dad's eyes. You were the first man who saw her and knew her and embraced her and celebrated her. *She will turn less to the counterfeit if she has experienced the real thing with you.*

We all know what it feels like when someone truly delights in us. We're drawn toward them. And when you look at your daughter and consistently make joy deposits into her heart and life, she will *become* that sparkle, that source of joy to you and others.

Yes, rough patches come and rough patches go, but if you press ahead in letting your reflection to her say, *"I delight in you,"* your loving truth will infiltrate even the hardest of calloused hearts. Though she seemingly may push you away at times, don't give up.

And if you don't have it in you to initiate and pursue (perhaps because it's not your style or you're tired of your daughter hurting or rejecting you), ask God to do it for you and through you. Remember that Jesus says that apart from Him you can do *nothing* (John 15:5).

Choose to Communicate with Her Today

Let your delight in her be pure and based on who she is as a girl, as a woman, created in the image of God, not based on what she can do or give or how she performs...or what she has done in the past.

Connect with your daughter today and tell her that you delight in her. Write, text, email, or call her to tell her this. She needs to hear it every day. (I know I'm being repetitive...because it's important.)

The most beautiful thing about my daughter is...

I will tell her this *today* by...

- ☐ speaking to her in person
- ☐ sending her a card in the mail
- ☐ texting her right now
- ☐ calling her on the phone (or Skype)
- ☐ writing her an email
- ☐ posting my words on her Facebook wall or on Instagram for all to see and read

CHAPTER 27

TOOL 14: CONVINCE HER SHE IS WORTHY

In the 2009 megahit movie *Avatar,* a consistent greeting is heard among the natives of the planet Pandora. When the Na'vi meet, they address each other with three simple words: "I see you."

More Than Ordinary Seeing

This phrase is much more than a simple hello. "I see you" is recognition of *more than ordinary seeing*. One source says, "What this acknowledgement means is simply *empathy.* It means that you acknowledge the other as one like yourself. It means that the 'I' and the 'You' are parts of a bigger whole." Though some may view this as a New Age concept, I choose to interpret it to mean that the only way any of us can clearly see another person is through the Holy Spirit inside us who reveals the truth of that person to us. Ask God for eyes to see who He created your daughter to be.

Seeing Yourself Through Someone Else's Eyes

The lead song of the soundtrack for the movie states, "I see me through your eyes." What a powerful way to put it. Restated in "dad-language": **Your daughter sees herself through your eyes.**

I truly believe that if you, dad, were to fully grasp this truth that *the way you see your daughter deeply impacts the way she sees herself,* it would shape every single interaction you have with her. You would be extra careful in the way you speak, react, discipline, engage, respond, reflect, listen, and comment.

If you could understand the magnitude of your verbal and nonverbal interactions with her, it would lead you to carefully consider *each and every response*, even on days when you feel overwhelmed by her Venusian ways.

If you truly understood the power of this life-changing truth, you would do everything possible *to convince your daughter that she is worthy.*

Let this concept now burrow its way into your soul in such a way that you will work hard to be quick to soften when wrong in order to keep her upright. Let it lead you to be quick to be strong when she needs your strength. And let it lead you to be quick to speak when she needs your words to water her thirsty soul. Day after day, month after month, year after year, she will see herself through your eyes.

Quick to Soften, to Be Strong, and to Speak

Tell her what you see that is good in her. She needs to know. Treasure her. Invest in her. Hold her heart with kid gloves.

Of course you see her for who she is, flaws and all. Yet she needs to be convinced by you that she is completely worthy of your love and your unconditional acceptance. Daily. In one way or another.

Girls Tell All About How Their Dads See Them

Speaking of dads seeing their daughters and the way it impacts them, I asked a few young women the following questions:

1. Does the way your dad sees you impact the way you see yourself? If so, then how? If not, why not?

Teenager: "Yes, because I know that my father has a good judgment of character, especially after the bad boy I dated."

Age 22 (single): "Absolutely. My dad is one of a few very important men in my life, and I value his opinion of me. When I am around him, I am sure to behave in ways that meet his approval. I seek and yearn for it."

Age 25 (single): "The impact used to be pretty huge. My father and I unfortunately do not have a very close relationship anymore. He communicates to me that my importance or worth in life has to do with my accomplishments and successes. I find myself seeing myself through the same lens—judging myself by my accomplishments and successes and trying to prove to others how good I am. It makes me wonder if that has rubbed off from him to me."

Every Girl Seeks the Approval of Her Father

Age 28 (single/engaged): "It definitely does. I think that every girl, myself included, no matter what stage of life you're in, seeks the approval of her father. He is the person who teaches you how to interact with boys/men, who teaches you how these boys/men will view you as a girl/woman. Even as an adult I can't help but instinctively return to my experiences with my dad for all of this."

Age 36 (married): "Yes, absolutely. When he says something complementary, now that I stop to think about it, it's like it touches me into my cells—strange but true. When he shows his delight in me, it warms my very core."

Age 42 (married): "In some ways yes and in some no. I know his approval overall means *so* much…the fact that he likes my husband means I made a right choice in choosing a good man…the fact that he loves my kids means so much to me as I feel I am doing a good job as a mom. The fact that he gets involved in my business makes me know he is proud of me being an entrepreneur."

2. Does your dad's view of you impact you more, less, or the same as other people's view of you?

Dad's View Compared to Others

Teenager: "His view impacts me in a different way than the views of my friends and peers. Only because I know that my dad won't always see eye to eye on how I act or the clothes I wear as my friends would since we are in a different generation, but I wouldn't say his view on me is less important. It's just important in a different way."

Age 22 (single): "My dad's view of me impacts me much more than other people's view of me. I see him as the most important man in my life right now, and his view is something very important to me."

Age 25 (single): "Probably less currently. Because of our unhealthy relationship, I have learned to have big boundaries with him. So his 'views' of me are many times dismissed. However, if I were to let them in, past my walls and boundaries, I think they would affect me a great deal and very negatively. I think more than others. I do actually long to be close to my father."

Age 28 (single/engaged): "Oh, so much more. His view of me has always impacted me and likely always will. I am able to walk away from the views of others without necessarily personalizing them. His views, spoken and unspoken, follow me into every relationship, job, major decision, and views of myself. I don't know if he knows all of this, but it's the truth."

Real Daugters. Real Responses. Real Longings

Age 36 (married): "I've never stopped to think about this. I guess because he sees me in a positive light, I've never had to feel defensive—I wonder if he didn't (see me positively), if I would have to grow a defense mechanism in order to less feel his poor view of me. I think it would send me into having to work really hard to prove him wrong. I'm glad that's not there with him."

Age 42 (married): "I would say more for sure. But my husband's view of me is *way* more important to me than my dad's."

So there it is. Real responses from real daughters.

She's Taking It All In

My hope is that your heart will absorb what you're reading in such a way that it guides you to be more aware of your invaluable role in your daughter's life. **Every single thing you do or say—or that you don't do or don't say—is impacting her positively or negatively.**

It may seem like I'm coming down hard on you. My intention is to inspire and motivate and challenge you to be more intentional with her because the more she sees that you delight in her, the more vibrant and alive she will be!

The way I will convince my daughter, both with words and actions, that I see her as worthy is...

CHAPTER 28

TOOL 15: TREAT HER LIKE A PRINCESS

Dad, whether you realize it or not, your daughter has been planning her wedding (or at least parts of it) since she was a little girl. This wishing and dreaming about the future seems to be hardwired genetically into most every girl.

I have had *countless interactions* with women over the years about romance and weddings. Girls *love* talking about this. (Just ask if she saw the royal wedding of Prince William and Catherine. Though some men may have thought it close to insanity, women across America were up at 3:00 a.m. watching it!)

Wishing and Hoping and Thinking and Praying

Do you remember that sixties song sung by Dusty Springfield called "Wishing and Hoping"? These words truly express the heart cry of many girls who are not only wishing and hoping for their Prince Charming to walk through the door, but they are thinking and praying and planning and dreaming every single night about being in his arms. (Yes, this can border on obsessive.)

As a young girl I remember loving to dress up as a bride and playing with bride dolls. Years later I spent beaucoup hours as a youth leader talking to girls about their dreams of having a boyfriend, finding Mr. Right, becoming engaged, the wedding, honeymoon, kids, and the "happily ever after." And now as a professional counselor, I wipe the tears of girl after girl who struggles in the post-breakup aftermath of being rejected or hurt emotionally to conclude that she will never, ever find someone who will "want her."

Girls Long to Be Chosen

All of this points to one universal fact: **Girls long to be chosen.** Most every girl wants to be *the beautiful princess who is chosen by the handsome* *prince*. There are always exceptions to every rule, but this is true for the majority of girls I've known.

Just think about television shows like *The Bachelor* and *The Bachelorette.* Despite a huge dose of drama and stupidity, millions of viewers tune in weekly to watch. Women across America are waiting to see who will get that final rose, the proposal, and the guy, while experiencing all of it vicariously. Being "the chosen one" drives the whole crazy adventure.

Girls Long to Know They're Worth Pursuing

This premise emerges time and again for girls, which underscores the fact that when a girl is picked by a boy, she radiates happiness and joy from the depths of her heart. She can't take the smile off her face when she finds out that the guy she likes actually likes her back. She believes that he is announcing to the world (her world) that she is *worth pursuing*.

This indescribable thing happens at the core of her being when she is wanted, desired, liked, pursued, enjoyed, accepted, loved, and chosen. She finally believes that she is enough.

So, as her dad, what do you do with this information? How can you compete with guys her age who seem to touch her heart in a way that yours may not be able to? I fully believe that as her dad, you not only have the role and the right but also the most amazing responsibility and privilege *to pursue her heart and choose her.* And when the boy you don't necessarily approve of tells your daughter that he will fight for her, be like one Abba Dad who recently said in response, "Well, I'm her dad and I'm going to fight even harder for her."

Activate, Protect, and Shield Her Heart

But this must happen over and over, daily and weekly and monthly. By doing so you will *activate, protect, and shield her heart.* By doing this you are modeling to her and teaching her what it *feels* like to be treated right by a guy.

The more you embrace her femininity by understanding her legitimate need for affirmation, letting her know that she is valuable and uniquely special (that's where the princess part comes in), the more emotionally healthy, stable, strong, resilient, and confident she will be.

She Is Your Princess (Royalty)

Let her know that she is your princess and that nothing she can do will ever take away her royal position in your life, in your family's life, or in your heart. Yes, you'll be disappointed at times when she makes decisions that aren't in line with yours, but above what she does, she needs to know that who she is remains secure. By taking her on dates and investing in her with your time, money, conversation, and energy, *you are placing value on her.*

Dad, remember that the little girl who used to delight you when she would twirl or sing or giggle or wrap her arms around your neck is now the young woman *who desperately needs you to be her handsome prince*, the one who fights for her, delights in her, affirms her, tells her she's beautiful, and still believes in her. Dr. John Sowers says it this way in *Fatherless Generation*:

Be Her Handsome Prince

> In the beginning, every girl longs to be Daddy's little girl. Daddy is the first man to whom she gives and from whom she receives love. Daddy is the man who shapes the way she sees herself. Daddy is the man who develops her worth and identity. She dreams of having his unspoiled attention. Dreams of forever being his precious little girl. Dreams of being the shining princess of his fairy-tale land.

Truth be told, I think the majority of girls would love to live in a palace with servants at their beck and call, donning ball gowns and tiaras, with travel options galore and power to influence and impact the world.

Strong, Amazing, Courageous, Beautiful Heroines

As you think about the movies your daughter loved as a girl, were any of them *Cinderella*, *Mulan*, or *The Little Mermaid*? And have any of the women in your life (wife, sister, friends) ever been drawn to *The Sound of Music*, *Pretty Woman*, *My Big Fat Greek Wedding*, *Star Wars*, *The Princess Bride*, or *The Matrix*? A common theme runs through every single one of them: **At the center of each of these stories is a strong, courageous, beautiful heroine.**

Whether that lead woman has a fairy-tale romance that sneaks up on her and changes her life forever or she's fiercely powerful and can kick someone's backside, the consistent thread is that the female lead is an *extraordinary woman who outshines everyone else*. I assume that movie producers either have some special insight about what lures us females into the box office or they simply know a *universal truth* common to all girls. I tend to think it's the latter.

Dad, make a conscious choice today to be your daughter's prince. Pursue her heart with as much energy and intention as you do tasks in your workplace.

Go After Her Heart in Warrior Fashion

Go after her heart in warrior fashion. And whether she's pushing you away or drawing you in, don't give up on letting her know she will always have a special place in your heart (romance) as your princess (royalty).

Let's think practically.

Find a chick flick and take your daughter to it *this week or next.* Afterward, talk with her about the romance in the movie. And on the off chance that royalty is included, listen to what her heart longs for. Ask her directly about that.

Then step in and treat her as she wants and deserves to be treated by a guy:

Open her door. Ask questions. Draw her out. Listen well.

PART THREE

Dialing In to Her Heart Needs

CHAPTER 29

UNDERSTANDING A GIRL'S ROMANTIC NEEDS

You just heard me say there's something universal in all of us girls that longs to be chosen by a guy. And because of that reality, we continually wish and pray that we will be *the one.*

Speaking of universal realities, in my thirty plus years of walking alongside teenage and twentysomething girls, one topic is a consistent theme: *boys*. I can't even begin to count the number of girls who have told me, "I want (or need) a boyfriend."

"I Want (or Need) a Boyfriend"

Let me say it another way: I have rarely met a teenage girl or young woman in her twenties who *hasn't* wanted a boyfriend.

I have watched girl after girl go to great lengths to get a guy to like her, even if it has meant changing her standards in order to present herself as someone she thinks a particular guy wants. Sometimes she starves herself or drinks at parties or dresses differently, even when it makes her uncomfortable. At other times she gives away her virginity, saying that it's "just one time," only to find herself caught in a pattern of "sharing" her body in order not to lose him.

This is where girls are extremely vulnerable because the female heart longs to be wooed and isn't always a wise discerner of the wooer.

A Bank and a Girl's Heart

Here's another way to think of it: We wouldn't risk putting our money in a bank that had no security behind it. Yet girls place themselves, their futures, and their self-worth into the hands of guys who often don't merit their trust and are an "insecure investment." All too often these girls are led in directions they don't want to go or later regret.

But once again, don't just take my word for it. Here are some responses from girls in their teens and twenties to the question: *What are your dreams and thoughts about what romance really looks like?* (Hint: This is what your daughter needs and wants from you.)

Real Responses from Girls About Romance

"To me romance looks like a man who pays attention to me. He listens to me when I talk, and he's willingly giving me attention. He notices what I like and does nice things for me. He surprises me. And he doesn't expect me to be anything but myself."

"Romance doesn't have to be a big gesture, although those things are nice too. I think it's the little everyday things that are the most romantic. Something to let you know that he's thinking about you every day—that means the most to me."

"I would love to fall in love with my best friend. To me that is what romance is. It is finding that person that sees you for who you are: stunningly beautiful, strong, driven, compassionate, loving, quirky, and perfect for them. If I find that someday, I can only imagine what I might feel. I know that this is how my God sees me, and I am *romanced* by Him."

"When a guy is sweet to you and treats you like you are the only beautiful girl on earth."

"My dreams and wishes are *way* out of possibility. I'm a *Twilight* fan *all* the way, and I wish there were a love like that—an intensity like that—that really existed."

"He is courteous, holding doors open, paying for the tab, etc. He wants to spend time with me. He wants to get to know me. **He likes me for who I am**—just as I am—both good and bad. He enjoys doing little things to show me that he cares about me (ex: an occasional flower maybe) but, more importantly, he tells me these things."

Dad, did you notice how very little money is involved in the things each girl said would make her feel romanced?

Unmet Core Needs Are Dangerous

I realize that we girls are sometimes demanding and seem like we want more than you as a dad can give. **But the truth is that we just want your attention and love and your heart turned toward us.** I'm seeking, as a woman, to give you a glimpse into the feminine soul, and I believe that when our core needs are not being met—safety and security, unconditional love and positive encouragement, and a sense of worth and value—we obsess on the externals.

Meet Her Real Needs

This is where you come in. As a dad, you will definitely dial in directly to your daughter when you look into her soul and help to meet her *real core needs.* Give your attention, your time, your patience, your money (remember that treasure and heart go hand in hand), your affirmation, and your tender heart responses (choosing this stance *is* being manly), which translates to authentic, active, amazing love.

You've probably heard it said that *intimacy* means "into-me-see." The girls in this chapter were all saying they want to be *seen* and *known* and *accepted* for who they are on the inside. This, in "girl-speak," means **we crave and need intimacy even though we usually focus more on romance.**

Connecting Her to the Real Need-Meeter

If a daughter truly *feels* loved by her dad (I'm talking about intense, unconditional, sacrificial, agape love), she will not be looking for it everywhere else. Taking this even deeper, you will be helping to direct her heart to receive love from her real Need-Meeter, her Abba Father God.

If your daughter's deepest need for love isn't being met authentically in a horizontal way (from you, her mom, others), as well as in a vertical way (from God), she may substitute the counterfeit (from a boy/man) for the real. She may fall for the scheme if she hasn't lived the true.

But it can get tricky because this isn't a foolproof formula guaranteeing that your daughter won't take the bait even if you are there for her. (I know this may be discouraging to hear, but I'm keeping it real.) Here's my story:

My Guy Story: There's Not a Foolproof Formula

I fell for the ploy, for the words, when he (the guy my parents prayed I wouldn't stay with) told me what I wanted to hear. He seemed to know my soft spots and how to get inside my head and heart in powerful ways. And as a woman created by God to be a responder, I accepted.

Yes, my dad loved me in tangible, real ways. But I still found myself drawn to an abusive guy (a Christian). Why? *Because he pursued me.* The problem was that he played mind games, gave me mixed messages, and was emotionally and mentally abusive. I changed so much about myself to be what he wanted. To illustrate, once after we broke up, I made a list of everything he'd told me he didn't like about me. I wrote down sixty-six things. Yet, after a two-month break, I started dating him again! I now understand that as a result of abuse from my grandfather, I held a deep-seated belief that I wasn't worth more than this. I was drawn to a guy who reinforced on the outside what I believed about myself on the inside.

My dad was there for me through it all. He got a lot of practice in wiping my tears and picking up the pieces of my broken heart. Both he and my mom wore out their knees praying for me (talking to God as opposed to talking to me) because they found that the more they tried to tell me to get out, the more I withdrew from them and attached to him. My dad never shamed me in the process of figuring it out the hard way. He somehow was there when I needed him.

Does Your Daughter Learn the Hard Way?

You may have a daughter like me who learns the hard way. I know your heart will break (or perhaps already has broken) over her poor romantic choices, and it's then that you feel helpless on many levels.

I can admit now that I looked to the guy I dated to somehow make me feel worthy and valuable. It backfired for one main reason: *As a finite human being, he couldn't give me something he didn't have to give.*

Here's how I explain this concept to girls when they look to a guy to meet their deepest needs. (Feel free to use this illustration with your daughter.)

Let's say you've just competed all afternoon in a track meet. The sun is blazing and you're dying of thirst. Someone offers you the choice of a big bottle of water or a chocolate milkshake. You take the milkshake because you love milkshakes, you love chocolate, and you're thirsty and hungry.

So how do you think you'll feel after you drink the milkshake? Sick to your stomach, most likely, and definitely thirsty, right?

But how can you be mad at the milkshake for not quenching your thirst when it was never intended to be a thirst quencher?

Guys Aren't Thirst Quenchers

Same thing with running to guys to meet your deepest needs. If you're thirsty for acceptance and love and meaning and identity, and you think you'll find that in a guy, you set yourself up for disappointment and disaster. You can't be mad at the guy for not quenching your thirst because God didn't make guys to be our thirst quenchers.

Only God can meet our deepest need!

And though this fact is absolutely 100 percent true, in the meantime, before we are filled up spiritually, *you, dad, are a close second* to having our deepest needs filled by God. **You help build a bridge for us to accept our Abba Father's love in a way that no other guy can because he's not our dad.** So for now, it's *you* who touch our hearts in ways we crave and need. When you love us in a pure way, it helps make God more approachable and less scary.

Let's Reminisce

Dad, think back to when your daughter was a little girl and delighted your heart, back when things were perhaps a bit less complicated.

Do you remember a time perhaps when you were reading the paper on a Saturday morning and she came bolting through the door crying because the older neighbor boys were being mean and she needed you to come outside and protect her? Somehow it wasn't as hard then to be inconvenienced as it is now that she's older. Her requests then were more straightforward and you could save the day fairly quickly and easily. Now her requests require more of your energy, time, money, and focus.

But she still longs to have you rescue her and save the day. In a girl's world, *that's romance.*

My next assignment is to help you reconnect to that heart place inside yourself so you can engage your daughter from that same place now. Your assignment here is going to be fun...I promise. But it will mean that you, the hero in this story, will have to take action.

Find a picture of your daughter from when she was around the age of four or five. Let yourself remember what she was like back then and what it felt like to enjoy her at that age. Make a copy of that picture, write a note on it, and then give it to her to let her know she was the apple of your eye then and always will be.

CHAPTER 30

ROMANCE AND ROYALTY: THE THREAT

Romance and *royalty*. I wonder what it is about these two concepts that strike a chord in most every girl regardless of her age, locale, ethnicity, or socioeconomic status. These themes are woven through the deepest places of her heart, tied together with a cord of vulnerability that is beautiful and fragile at the same time.

Being Chosen = Being the Prize

Perhaps one of the reasons we girls are drawn to romance and royalty is that God made us that way. We seem to have this intense, legitimate desire to feel beautiful and unique, worthy and valuable, loved and adored. Sadly, though, we often don't feel as though we're *pretty enough* or *good enough* or *quality enough* unless a guy says it's true. And we think that if we are chosen by a guy or if we have the title of *girlfriend* or *wife*, then it announces to all of creation that we are prized, *his prize.*

Here is where the plot thickens.

As in most every story, there is a villain or nemesis who wants to destroy the main character. Whether it's the wicked witch in *The Wizard of Oz* or the Dark Lords of the Sith battling the Jedi in *Star Wars*, part of the intensity of a storyline is the conflict between one side and the other, *all in an attempt to destroy or overpower the lead, the hero, the star of the show.*

The Enemy Has a Clear Agenda and It Ain't Pretty

The Bible tells us that we have an enemy who *prowls around* like a roaring lion seeking someone he may cuddle up to. *No, that's not how the verse reads!* This enemy, as 1 Peter 5:8 tells us, has a name: devil. And he is "looking for someone to *devour*." Those are fighting words. Our enemy isn't looking for a cuddle buddy. He's out for destruction.

Jesus said this enemy is a thief who "comes only to steal and kill and destroy" (John 10:10). His intent is to destroy each of us, the main characters in our life story, the story that God is writing. And because he can't hit God directly, he goes after anyone associated or related to Him.

Additionally, Satan is called "a liar and the father of lies" (John 8:44). I would have thought he'd be called "the father of evil" or even "the father of darkness." But as "the father of lies," this means he specializes in one thing: *lies.* And his number one goal is to get us to believe his lies. He wants us, God's image bearers, to believe lies about God, ourselves, others, our bodies, relationships, boundaries, and the world around us. *He lies about everything.*

Further, if he can persuade your daughter to believe his villainous lies as he attempts to tear her down, steal her joy, and come against her true self, this will rob her of being fully alive as a woman who can impact the lives of others with her one-of-a-kind uniqueness.

Assault on Her Heart

You need to be aware of the enemy's agenda and plan of attack against your daughter. He's real, he's out for blood, and his scheme against her is completely opposite of God's heart for her. As her Creator, God has a desire to see her become more like Him so that she can fully be who He has designed her to be.

The enemy hates that plan. And he's not going to watch it unfold without doing everything in his power to thwart it and to spoil her beautiful story. In the book *Captivating,* John and Stasi Eldredge say it this way:

> If you listen carefully to any woman's story, you will hear a theme: the assault on her heart. We don't believe we are beautiful, so we work hard to be outwardly beautiful or we "let ourselves go" and hide behind a persona that has no allure. We try so hard, in so many ways, to protect our hearts from further pain.

The Enemy's Agenda Against Your Daughter

In Ezekiel 28 we read that the king of Tyre was "the seal of *perfection,* full of *wisdom* and perfect in *beauty*" (v. 11). Some interpret this as a veiled reference to Satan as the true force behind Tyre's king. If so, this passage captures what the devil lost when he was kicked out of heaven. From the time he was stripped of his position of power and dignity as an angelic being until now, he has gone after women in three areas:

1. not feeling *perfect* enough
2. not feeling *smart* enough
3. not feeling *beautiful* enough

We women are vulnerable at the places where we strive to be perfect enough, where we want to be smart enough, where we long to be beautiful enough, where we ache to be loved (romance), where we wish to be chosen, and where we dream of being valued, unique, and special (royalty). And to state the obvious, this "*not enough*" theme is rarely dominant or debilitating in men, but it is rampant among women.

"Not Enough" Theme Runs Rampant Among Women

If you want to be empowered as a dad to stand in the gap for your daughter and with your daughter, I urge you to heed the following:

- *Be aware of your enemy.*
- *More importantly, know the One who is stronger and more powerful.*

The best news of all is that Satan is a defeated enemy, and his ultimate destination is the lake of fire (Revelation 20:7-10). But until that time, he is having a heyday.

(Some of you may be uncomfortable right now with all the spiritual talk about this enemy, the devil. My intent is not to make you uncomfortable; my intent is to present truth from the Bible that will serve as a foundation for you to fight as a spiritual warrior for your daughter.)

Your daughter needs you to fight spiritually for her. Contend for her in prayer so that God's healing truth can reach her soul despite the enemy's attempts to derail her from connecting to that truth. And in a world that presents the counterfeit, the best way to stand strong is to be rooted and grounded in absolute truth, God's Word.

Dad, become a man of God's Word if you aren't one already. Here's an idea for how you might start that process:

Become a Man of God's Word

- Write out one to two verses that contain promises you claim for your daughter.
- Put her name in each verse as you personalize it.
- Start with Psalm 91 and 139 if you need a place to begin.

When you align with God's own words and press Him to keep His promises, He will respond out of His love relationship with you.

Be a Prayer Warrior and a Truth Warrior

Dad, be the warrior that you want to be and that your daughter needs you to be. Be a prayer warrior and a truth warrior. Every day, let your daughter know that she is:

- accepted just the way she is (remind her that she is in process and processes take time)
- smart (IQ isn't the only way to measure intelligence; there are many kinds of "smarts"—emotional, musical, interpersonal, artistic, and spiritual, for example)
- beautiful (beauty comes in all shapes and sizes, with variances of uniqueness that add flair and fun)

The area where my daughter is most vulnerable to attack is (low self-esteem, lacking confidence, eating disorder, verbal abuse from other girls, relationships with guys, weak boundaries, drugs or alcohol, other)...

My spiritual plan of attack to protect her today is...

CHAPTER 31

ROMANCE AND ROYALTY: THE GIRLS TELL ALL

I want you now to hear from girls between the ages of thirteen and thirty as they give you a glimpse inside their minds and hearts on this theme of romance and royalty. This will not only give you insight into what your daughter may be thinking and feeling, but you *can use these questions to open conversations with her.*

Messages from Movies

Question 1:
What messages about being a girl and being pretty or beautiful have you heard from the movies you watched?

"I do not appreciate what 'the world' dictates as beautiful. I do not appreciate the expectation that movies and celebrities put on us girls to be thin, covered in makeup, always do our hair a certain way, whiten our teeth, wear the right brands of clothing, etc."

"I didn't really care when I was a kid, and I didn't care 'til I didn't fit the accepted norm, which has been the last couple of years. **I think I'm pretty, but I do wish my body looked different.** If I'm not a size two in stilettos and a pencil skirt, will I still find the perfect man?"

"I learned that you had to be physically beautiful to obtain those princess dreams."

Disney Princesses Speak

"I had a conversation with one of my friends recently while we were watching *The Princess and the Frog* about what princesses we are most like now. She told me I was a combination of Ariel and Belle: Belle because I am beautiful and Ariel because I am stubborn."

"Being pretty is very important. It takes you a distance in life. It's not fair, but it's true. Being feminine is beautiful and valuable."

"You have to be able to sing and dance well. The usual, like you have to be skinny and beautiful and kind to everyone. And that you need a man to save you (totally kidding on that last part, but that is kind of what Disney movies teach)."

"The Beautiful Get It All, Have It All"

"Girls have to dress provocatively or scandalously in order to catch a man's attention—showing more skin is good. I don't like that idea, and try my best not to conform to it. . .but it does make me wonder if those portrayals are a reality."

"It seems that being pretty or beautiful is a necessary trait of being viewed as a princess. **Movies tend to portray that the beautiful ones are the ones who get pursued and are desired."**

Question 2:

Now that you're older, do you ever think about being a princess? If you did bring "the princess" back into your life, how would it impact you?

"I think everyone wishes they could be royalty at some point or another."

"A Prince Would Definitely Marry You"

"I guess I don't label it as being a princess, but I guess I do when I think about feeling empowered and deserving of being treated well. **If I did bring the princess back, I guess I would be the woman I dream about being.** I wouldn't worry about doing the wrong thing or being judged. It would be liberating."

"Love yourself, just like the princesses loved themselves and weren't afraid to show their beauty."

"I think it's impossible working with little kids constantly not to think about this every once in a while. Just the other day I was playing makeup with a four-year-old girl and an eight-year-old girl, and after the older one was done applying all my 'beautiful' makeup, the younger one says, 'Oh wow, you look pretty. A prince would definitely marry you.'"

"I never think about being a princess. I do think about dressing up really nice and having a fun event to go to where I have a date and I'm wearing something far more formal than I would typically."

"I do not so much think about being a princess. However, I do think that often the same concept does cross my mind frequently. **The idea that I want to be beautiful, desired, wanted, and known is still something that I think about."**

"If I were to bring 'the princess' back into my life, I think I would try a lot harder to portray beauty externally. However, I think that would have a negative impact on who I have become now and on the person that I am growing to be content with."

"No, no, no. I do not—for whatever reason—have any desire to be a princess or anything of the sort."

Question 3:

Can you think of any way that your dad could make you feel more like royalty, like a princess?

"Maybe reach out to see how I'm doing more consistently instead of the other way around."

"My dad already treats me that way. I'm his little girl, always."

"I think one of the biggest things, and I'm not saying he fails to do this by any means, is that he helps me to see my strength, my beauty, my talent, my uniqueness, and that he shows me that I am a woman to be cherished and pursued by doing just that. **Anything my dad does to just let me know he is thinking about me or wants to spend time with me means a lot and makes me feel honored, like a princess."**

Dad Was There but Not There

"Maybe talking to me would be a good start. I know my dad works really hard and carries a lot of stress, and this last year has had a lot of illness. But growing up when I would talk to him, try and confide in him, and ask for advice, it was always like he was somewhere else. And even though I asked him a direct question, he wouldn't even answer. He probably didn't even hear me over whatever he was stressing about. But it would have been nice to know he heard me, to know that what I had to say was important to him, whether or not he cared about the subject. I struggle a lot with the need to be heard and having my words honored as an adult. If I had known that what I had to say was important, I might feel more important and confident. And unlike the other women in his life, I actually wanted to have a conversation and not just talk at him. **I want to exchange ideas and learn from him."**

Question 4:

If your dad were to fill up your love tank by making you feel loved and special and accepted and enjoyed, what could he do specifically to make you feel those things now in your life?

"Laugh out loud more. My dad has so much stress, and so I try to make him laugh. He might smile, but when he laughs I do feel special and that he enjoys me."

Needing Positive Reinforcement

"Embrace my individual attributes. I don't want to be like anyone else and you don't want a robot for a daughter. Don't tell me what not to do. Positive reinforcement is so much more effective. I worry about doing something my father told me not to do, and I think if I do these things, a man isn't going to want me."

"To hear him say that I'm beautiful would be great. I've never heard him remark on my appearance in a positive way."

"My dad is too far away from this. I'm sorry, it just doesn't even seem reachable to me."

"My love tank is pretty full as far as my parents go. My dad is very good about hugging me and telling me he loves me. He's also very good about doing things for me when I ask and taking an interest in my life."

"Encourage my dreams—no matter how outlandish or even if it's not the dream you have for your daughter. I could have been the next Mariah Carey if I really wanted, or I could have been the best ballerina, but no one listened."

"Encourage My Dreams"

"My dad could take me somewhere spontaneously or planned, and pursue me and allow me to pursue him. I am excited for the day when we can look at each other and really know one another. Right now it feels like we pretend, but are really going in two different directions."

"He always seems too busy with his laptop or his blackberry or his cell phone to enjoy a conversation with me. He's a great listener, but I wonder if he just does it so I'll eventually shut up. When I try to ask about him, he doesn't want to talk about it. I'd love for him to open up about his life in an honest and real way. **I want him to be present."**

"I Want Him to Be Present"

"Talk to me, encourage me to seek my passions without dampening the vision with too much practicality."

"I think the best a dad could do is to maybe verbally express what he thinks of me (whether that is internal beauty or external beauty)."

"The only thing that I can think of for my dad is accepting me completely as I am...flaws and all. He already is the most amazing person I know."

"He could just out of nowhere, and for no reason other than to make me feel those things, send a little letter or note or message saying that he loves me, thinks I am special, accepts me, and enjoys who I am."

"What You Think About Me Matters"

"Just to hear his honesty about what he thinks about me and when he thinks about me makes me feel all of those things."

The two comments from these daughters that touch my heart the most, the ones that will motivate me to action are...

1.

2.

It's time for your next dad-daughter date. For this date, you have the incredible opportunity to make your daughter feel like a princess who is adored by her handsome prince (Dad, that's you!). Have fun. See the appendix for **"Date 6: Dad to Daughter Questions on Romance and Royalty."**

CHAPTER 32

HELP HER FIGURE OUT WHO SHE IS

If you've ever been involved in a construction project, you know how critically important a solid foundation is to the whole house. This chapter addresses the underlying structure of your daughter's "house" that impacts her relationship with herself and with boys.

To best understand your daughter's motivations, drives, and needs, let's consider what one expert describes as the natural and healthy psychosocial tasks between adolescence and young adulthood. This will give you an idea of what is "normal" based on her age.

Psychologist Erik Erikson says the key developmental life tasks during adolescence (ages twelve to twenty) are to wrestle through and figure out "identity vs. role confusion."

Her Who Versus Her Do

Identity = Who am I?
Role Confusion = Where do I fit?

Let's explore the ways you can help her answer these two main questions about her identity and her role in life.

How will she figure out who she is?

How to Help Her Decode Who She Is

1. By internalizing truth about her positive enduring qualities that exist regardless of performance, success, perfection, or outcome.

2. By not letting her mistakes define her or hold her back, but instead using them as steppingstones for learning (not shaming).
3. By having consistent reminders that she is valued and worthy just because she is, no matter what she does or doesn't do right.
4. By knowing *and believing* that she has a purpose here to fulfill (this will come only as truth is reinforced through both horizontal and vertical relationships).

How to Help Her Figure Out Where She Fits

How will she figure out where she fits?

1. By trying on different hats and seeing which ones fit her best.
2. Through support from those around her who remind her not to give up until she finds her niche, her passion, her calling.
3. By learning to be patient with herself through trial and error, something she'll easily forget unless she's told time and again.
4. By not being pressured to figure things out before she's ready, yet feeling loved, encouraged, and supported through the obstacle course of her life.

Erikson describes the next stage of psychosocial development during young adulthood (ages nineteen to forty) as the time to keep wrestling and continue figuring out the tasks of "intimacy vs. isolation."

Knowing Versus Connecting

Intimacy = Who knows me?
Isolation = Who do I connect with?

10 Things She Needs from You and Others

How will she figure out who to know and who to let know her, as well as who to let in or not let in to her soul and her life?

1. By being **encouraged to trust her intuition and gut sense** about things even if she can't always put words to why something does or doesn't sit right. *(Dads, make sure to never*

make fun of her intuitive sense because she will use that same skill with guys as she assesses their motives and character.)

2. By having experiences with her mom and dad that **let her know what it's like to be fully known and accepted.** Then from that place of security, to be cheered on to adventure, knowing she is okay.

3. By being accustomed to **expressing her thoughts, feelings, opinions, needs, interests, viewpoints, tastes, preferences, likes, dislikes,** thus perpetuating a pattern of self-disclosure that is built on a foundation of self-confidence.
4. By being in relationships inside and outside the family where she has **the freedom to say both yes and no.**
5. Through **using her gifts and talents to touch the world** around her while seeing that her life has impact and meaning outside of herself. (She will need your support to step out in new ways.)
6. By **connecting with you, dad,** as her first experience of male interaction and depth, thus leaving her less emotionally vulnerable and needy for male attention, love, acceptance, and validation.
7. By **connecting with her mom** as her first experience of female depth, interaction, honesty, dependence, and interdependence to provide a solid foundation for embracing her own femaleness.
8. By being **unconditionally accepted and guided** through the process of understanding her hormonal and emotional fluctuations that influence both her decision making and her responses.
9. By being **loved, pursued, enjoyed, and known by you, dad,** before any other boy influences her fragile yet strong heart.
10. By having the assurance that **she can always come home to vent, talk, learn, and get her love tank filled up by you, dad.**

Though this list may seem overwhelming to activate, I encourage you to choose one to work on, knowing that your example will set the foundation for the kind of guy she'll date.

Her foundational need that I will help meet today is...

CHAPTER 33

PREPARING HER FOR DATING

When it comes to preparing your daughter to launch into the world of dating and relating to the boys in her life, if you know what she needs (even if she doesn't), you will be better able to guide her through the maze.

What Her Heart Needs

She needs to be:

- *seen* (noticed)
- *heard* (listened to)
- *communicated with* (talked with...she needs words)
- *desired* (wanted)
- *pursued* (this confirms her worth)
- *adored* (made to feel special, important, unique)
- *enjoyed* (laughed with, have fun with)
- *respected* (valued)
- *loved* (treasured)
- *esteemed* (honored)

Every girl I've ever known has longed for all ten of these things. But despite these clear longings, I'm amazed at how often girls settle for less when it comes to the guys they choose to date.

She Will Internalize a Failed Relationship

It's easy for girls to receive and experience these things during the "honeymoon" stage in a dating relationship (which is about two months maximum), only to then have them stop or diminish, causing the girl either to believe that *she* is deficient or that something is wrong with her because *she* wasn't enough to hold his gaze.

Another common thing I hear from girls is how often they abandon these ideals after finding that very few guys consistently have it in them to give these things anyway, often leading her then to "settle" or lower her bar (or standard) while giving up on her dreams of a great relationship. Or she finally realizes the guy had a hidden agenda from the start and only gave these things as a way to use her.

Then once a girl's heart has been broken and she feels like used or damaged goods, she typically keeps **repeating her patterns** by choosing similar guys with hope for a different outcome (though that rarely happens). Or she **internalizes projected negative beliefs** from the stupid guy and turns against herself with a huge pile of blame added as a garnish.

So what does this mean to you as a dad? **How can you actively prepare your daughter to choose a good guy?**

You, Dad, Get to Set the Guy Standard

- *Treat her* the way you want a guy to treat her.
- *Treat her mom* the way you want a guy to treat her. (Your model is one she will follow, and you can do this, even if there has been divorce, by not bad-mouthing her mom.)
- *Ask forgiveness* when you've blown it.
- *Draw her out*—listen to her, talk to her, invest time in her.
- *Treasure her* by investing money in things important to her.
- *Compliment her* and tell her *often* she is beautiful to you.
- *Value her mind* by discussing things she's interested in.
- *Teach her* about things she wants to learn from you, ranging from how to be treated by a guy to car maintenance, house repair, sports tips and techniques, money interests, etc.
- *Encourage her* to learn from her mistakes by kindly and gently helping her process the good, the bad, and the ugly.
- *Support her goals* and *respect her decisions* even if they're different from yours.
- *Be there* to work through the ups and downs with her (without shaming her in the "process of processing").

Speaking of setting a solid foundation, I love what Kevin, a former Abba Project Dad, had to say: "I've turned a corner. Both of my daughters have new boyfriends now, and *I just forced them to come meet me*. I wouldn't have done that a year ago." Kevin looked those boys in the eyes and let them know that he was essentially going to be looking over their shoulders. This is what being a dialed-in dad looks like in action!

My friend Felicia is a gifted counselor in Indiana. I met her at a conference when I spoke on the value of a dad's influence in his daughter's life. Immediately after the event, she contacted a number of dads whose daughters (between the ages of five and twelve) were her clients, and began her own dads' group. Felicia shared something profound with me about the value of dads inviting their daughters into their lives to give them a future model for relating to men:

Wise Words from a Wise Counselor

> I challenged the dads to do things with their daughters—guy things. Most of the dads hadn't ever thought of doing a masculine thing with their daughters, but the girls were pretty excited about their dads teaching them things they like to do. I suggested that the dads take their daughters into their workshop when working on their car and plan a day to go fishing with them.
>
> I always, always drill this with dads in family counseling. I tell them, "You are your daughter's only teacher about what to look for in a husband. She needs to know what men are like and see what you do." I believe it's easy for dads to push daughters aside when they clean the gutters and change the oil. But I tell them, "Your girls need to see your lives too."

The thing I want to teach my daughter that I've never taught her before is...

CHAPTER 34

DADS, DUDES, AND DUDS: A DAD TELLS ALL

Near the end of my first group of The Abba Project, I asked the dads if there was any topic they wanted me to cover that we hadn't yet discussed. The unanimous vote was for me to answer the question: **What do we do when our daughter is dating a guy we don't like or don't think is good for her?**

What Do We Do When Our Daughter Is Dating a Guy We Don't Like?

This question initially came from one of the dads whose twentysomething daughter was dating a guy that he and his wife really didn't care for. And what I can tell you, after more than three decades of interacting with families, is that this dilemma has come up more times than I can count. It's never easy on anyone, parents or kids.

One of the biggest mistakes I see parents make is to get into *power struggles* with their girls over boyfriends. Girls can easily put their hearts before their brains when it comes to boys, and it's not so easy for a heart to do a 180-degree turn once it's set in a certain direction. This is where conflicts arise.

If your daughter is under the age of eighteen, you have more power to impact her choices because she is under your roof. **But *power* is a relative term.** The truth is that she will go behind your back and do what she wants to do based on what *she thinks* is best for her, and you can't always stop her.

Power Is a Relative Term

Here is Mark's story.

A lesson learned from one Abba Project Dad

My wife and I went through a period of time (six years) of fighting for our daughter with one unbelievably horrible relationship she had. We

Mark's Story

were completely rational (we thought) telling her what a no-good rotten scumbag he was (and he was), and how we would *never* let him be a part of anything we did as a family.

Well, that did not work very well at all. Actually, it drove us farther apart. We realized that we could not control her choices. We needed to love her and be there to pick up the pieces as she saw what her choices were doing to her. We needed to love her unconditionally.

None of this was easy. There were many days I could not understand how this could be happening. But I could not give up on my daughter.

With the help of Michelle and The Abba Project, we learned something life-changing.

I began sharing (in a loving way) the qualities that we desired for her to have in a relationship and ultimately a marriage. Qualities that include honesty, respect, trust, caring, someone that put her needs above his always, and someone who would lay his life down for her. I also pointed out great examples of healthy relationships that were being modeled by two of her siblings at the time; that had a huge impact too.

It has been an ongoing intentional investment of time in strengthening our relationship through date nights (with me), text messages, emails, and phone calls while sharing our unconditional love (that we know comes from above) that has caused a miraculous change in our daughter's life.

What kind of relationship do you want with your daughter while she is figuring out what she likes and doesn't like, what she thinks and wants and needs?

Don't Leave It Up to Mom

Make sure not to choose a passive stance, defaulting to excuses such as, *"I'll let her mom deal with this,"* or *"She's got her mind made up and I'll trust her to figure it out."* Simply saying you trust her isn't enough. Sometimes I've wondered if dads say this to their daughters as a way to avoid an uncomfortable conversation or to bypass setting limits that will probably erupt into an argument or standoff.

To put it frankly, your daughter will like (and date) whomever she wants to like (and date) no matter what you say. If she thinks you don't like him, she will simply hide the relationship from you. So it all comes down to whether you want to keep your relationship with her strong and open through her process of figuring things out or you want to let her figure it out on her own without your input (not recommended, of course).

Remember that her frontal lobe where she does all her thinking, decision making, and reasoning isn't fully developed until she is twenty-five. *She needs your input even if she doesn't think she does.*

I've seen many parents alienate their daughter when she's dating a guy who is not their choice. Clearly the age of the girl plays a part here, but as a general rule, she is going to have to decide what kind of guy is right for her. And she will do it with or without your help. I know it's hard to see beyond the current struggle, but when it's not a black-and-white issue (unless he's abusive or involved in illegal or unethical practices), a key question for you to ask yourself is:

What do I want my forever relationship with her to look like?

I'm not saying that she doesn't need your input, because if you say nothing then she doesn't have your perspective or insight. But if you only criticize and put her boyfriend down, she will run to him because "he understands and 'gets me' and gives me space to be me." She will interpret anything negative you say about him as an attack on her because she hears you saying that she has bad taste and can't choose well. This is when a girl gets better at hiding what she's doing with him if her heart isn't convinced he's not good for her.

Your Forever Relationship

Here are a few practical questions, dad, for you to consider:

Do the Math

Dad: Do you talk *at* her, telling her what you don't like about him?

Dude: Does he listen to her and side with her?

Do the math: Who will she choose to spend time with?

Dad: Do you pull back out of disgust, anger, or disappointment?

Dude: Does he move toward her, embracing her, holding her?

Do the math: Who will she choose to spend time with?

Dad: Do you put walls up in your interactions with her to protect your hurting heart over her choice with this guy?

Dude: Does he provide emotional support to lift her up and encourage her while she's processing hurt and sadness from you?

Do the math: Who will she choose to spend time with?

Let Your Actions Speak Louder

If I had one piece of advice to give you dads if your daughter is dating a guy you don't like, it is: **Let your actions speak louder than your words. Words are key, but keep them few. Use your words wisely and sparingly. But do use words. (Silence is not an option.)**

Being careful when you speak is one idea that goes a long way if your daughter is rebelling through this stage of separating and individuating or dating a guy you don't approve of.

Treat Her the Way You Want a Guy to Treat Her

And I guess I do have another piece of advice: **treat her the way you want a guy to treat her.** As I said earlier, because more is caught than taught, **be the kind of man you want her to marry.**

Let her experience real love from you. It will provide a good template for comparison. Here are a few more takeaways:

How to Care for Your Daughter's Heart

- Spend *more time* with her during her datable years.
- Take her on dates (weekly or at least bimonthly).
- Model to her what it *looks* like and *feels* like to be treated well by a guy (you).
- Respect her with your words and actions.

She will remember how you interact with her more than any lecture you give.

She will compare the way you treat her to the way her boyfriend treats her (even if she never admits it).

CHAPTER 35

DADS, DUDES, AND DUDS: SHE NEEDS YOU TO FIGHT FOR HER

My friend Bill recently posted this comment on his Facebook wall:

> Teenage Guys: Please keep in mind that comments referring to sexual activity regarding my daughter may very well result in your crash course that this dad can and will seriously whoop you. Seriously.

Stand in the Gap for Your Daughter

This comment prompted me to ask Bill for the backstory. With his daughter's permission he eagerly wrote out the story, one that demonstrates the importance of a dad protecting his teenage daughter in a day when sexual talk and innuendo is the norm for kids. I trust his story will inspire you to stand in the gap for your daughters, whether it embarrasses her or not.

Bill's Story

I have three kids: a son who is married and two daughters. One daughter is twenty-two and married, and one is fifteen and a freshman in high school. The message I wrote on Facebook is regarding a comment made on a Facebook post after my youngest daughter simply posted "I'm ready to do something." I started to "like" her post when I noticed a "friend" of hers, a guy about sixteen, commented, "Something sexual?"

Needless to say, my dadness kicked in, and I thank God the ignorant, hormone-infested sixteen-year-old guy was not in my presence at that moment. Having been a teenage guy at one point in my life (many, many years ago), I knew what was going through his mind, and it infuriated me even more. I have always been highly protective by nature, and especially so with my family and even more so with my girls.

My wife and I have always stayed in our kids "personal space" and monitored email, texts, Facebook, etc. To some, it may seem like such a small thing—but guarding the honor and purity of our daughters is something that we only get one shot at.

I watch guys as I'm out with my daughters, not in a paranoid way, just in a watchful and protective manner. I have taught my girls to be aware of their surroundings and be aware of even body language so that hopefully they could recognize a potentially bad situation and avoid it without causing a scene.

We stay plugged in to what our youngest daughter is involved in. Who her friends are. Everything. Sometimes she gets really mad at me. I don't mind. I have told all of my kids that I'm their dad first and their buddy second. But we have also told them (and tell them regularly) that we love them and that we get one chance to raise them up in the way they should go.

What I can tell you for sure is that I'm not going to miss the opportunity to be the best dad I can be.

Five Tips on Navigating the Guy Thing

Here are some additional ideas on navigating "the guy thing" with your daughter:

1. **Hang in there and be ready to speak up when she opens a window.** By intentionally pursuing opportunities to talk with her one-on-one, it will result in times when she will open up and other times when she won't. Don't give up. Keep pursuing her heart.
2. **She needs your input, but wait for her to ask for your opinion.**
3. She will ask for your input more frequently and with less resistance if you've **already been building a solid relationship with her before, during, and after guys come in and out of her life.**
4. **Guard your tongue carefully. Don't say things you'll regret.** (Like the adage says, the one we all heard our parents tell

us, "*think before you speak.*") And when she does ask for your thoughts, try to say less rather than more. If you give her just one or two things to consider, she will more easily digest it without being overwhelmed or defensive.

5. **Ask her questions that allow her to feel your support** rather than your third degree. Teach her *how* to think, not just *what* to think.

These questions can't come all in one sitting, but here are some questions you could ask your daughter about the guy she may be interested in:

Questions to Teach Her *How* to Think

- Tell me what you like/love about him? (This way you start with something positive.)
- What does he like/love about you?
- How does he let you know he enjoys you?
- What do you laugh about when you're together?
- Tell me about his family.
- What is his relationship like with his mother/father/siblings?
- What does he want to be when he "grows up"?

(She may get defensive with these next ones so be careful to watch your tone so that you aren't asking with an air of judgment.)

- How free are you to use your voice with him?
- Do you have any concerns about him as a person (his present/past)?
- If there was one thing about him you could change, what would it be?
- Where do your spiritual beliefs match up and where do they differ?
- What degree (or educational goals) does he have?
- How do you both navigate conflict when you disagree or differ in your opinions/choices?

Pace with Her, Not Barrels Loaded

These are heavy questions, which is why, depending on where your relationship is with your daughter, you may be able to ask only one or two of them at a time. Yet these questions will give you a template to work from over time in order to draw her out.

And if your daughter is in a relationship that currently breaks your heart, I encourage you to write out (yes, literally *write out*) a list of specific

Talk Upward

and measureable prayer requests. Watch God work as you use your voice to advocate on your daughter's behalf with Abba Father God.

And if necessary, you also may need to sit down with the guy and ask him not to see your daughter anymore. One Abba Dad did this and told his daughter that it's his job to protect her heart. I'll get you his number if you need a pep talk!

Through the centuries couples have married without parental blessing or support. Sometimes the outcome has been good, sometimes not. But if the guy your daughter has chosen isn't someone you like, the difficult but necessary question to ask yourself is:

How can I maintain a quality relationship with my daughter even if I don't like the choice she is making with this guy?

The two things I am taking away from this chapter are...

1.

2.

(If your daughter isn't yet old enough to date, use this space to write out a prayer or a statement about what kind of guy you want her to be drawn to down the road.)

It's time to go on your seventh date with your daughter. Whether or not she has started dating, this date with you is going to open up some great conversations. See the appendix for **"Date 7: Dad to Daughter Questions on Guys, Dating, and Relationships."**

CHAPTER 36

THE SEX TALK: THE NUMBERS TELL ALL

You might be wondering why I'm including a chapter on the importance of talking to your daughter about sex. Here is my response, plain and simple: **If you don't talk to her about sex, she's going to learn about it everywhere and anywhere else.**

You have to ask yourself whether her teachers will be popular magazines, the entertainment industry, and her peers (who are all no better qualified to weigh in on this issue than she is), or whether it will be *you*. She needs you to speak into her life about this topic.

You, Dad, Have to Lead the Way

A recent study found that six in ten Americans believe that it is "extremely important" for fathers to lead their children by providing them with morals and values. Add in the fact that nine in ten teenagers say they would delay sexual activity and avoid teen pregnancy if they could have more open, honest conversations about these things with their parents, and it makes the point clear: **You, dad, have to lead the way in dialoguing with your daughter about this issue.**

Stating the obvious a bit more bluntly, *I believe that if girls stopped opening their legs, our entire country would change.*

Looking for Love in All the Wrong Places

Think about it. If girls stopped "looking for love in all the wrong places" (can you hear the song in your head?) instead of running from guy to guy in an attempt to fill their love tanks or numb their pain (often from dad deficits), *it would change everything*. Numbers would go down—numbers of unwanted pregnancies, abortions (incidentally, I have yet to meet a woman without a forever scar because of an abortion), heartbreak after breakups, and money spent on the thriving sex industry, to name a few.

Legitimate Need, Illegitimate Fix

When a woman has significant dad wounds or dad voids due to him not being there either physically or emotionally, she will look elsewhere because she has a legitimate, God-given need for love. And if she doesn't get her real need for love met in a legitimate way by her dad (and her heavenly Dad), she will accept an illegitimate, temporary counterfeit if that's all that's available.

Maurice Hilliard was an assistant women's basketball coach at Pepperdine University and wrote a book titled *The Price of a Pearl.* As a coach he often found himself unexpectedly designated to a "dad role" with girls on his team. Sometimes this came at the urgent request of the girls' moms and at other times by default when girls had no other male to turn to as a guide, confidant, and mentor. He conducted a survey of 720 teenage girls and found that:

- 97 percent of the girls said that having parents they could talk to could help reduce teen pregnancy.
- 93 percent said that having loving parents they could talk to reduced their own risk of teen pregnancy.
- 76 percent said that their fathers were very or somewhat influential in their decision whether to have sex.

Fathers Are Key Influencers on a Daughter's Decision to Have Sex

Many potential factors could influence this last statistic about a father's influence on his daughter's sexual choices. I posit a few possibilities:

- *Dad's personal example* and what he models with his own life decisions, whether positive or negative
- *Conversations (or lack of) from dad to daughter about faith and spirituality* with regards to sex
- *Dad not talking about potential pitfalls*, thus leaving his daughter to navigate on her own through the intensity of our highly sexualized culture
- *Dad's own unhealthy sexualized behaviors*, including pornography, sex addiction, or toxic verbiage about sex and women
- *Dad's absence*, either due to divorce or his work schedule or lifestyle
- *Dad exhibits extreme discomfort* when talking about this subject, possibly due to sexual abuse in his past or growing up in a home where this topic was off limits, for example

Regardless of the reason for talking or not talking with your daughter, **it's essential that you, dad, make a decision to push past the discomfort and engage your daughter in honest conversation about sex.**

Push Past the Discomfort and Talk with Her

And as if those earlier stats weren't enough, here is further information based on cutting-edge research from the National Campaign to Prevent Teen and Unplanned Pregnancy. I encourage you to show these statistics to your daughter as a way to open up dialogue with her on this subject. Because concrete data will help her to *get into her head*, this information can guide her to *think* about this issue rather than to merely react from an emotional place.

- ***Six in ten teens* who have had sex say they wish they had waited.** (This is a key statistic to tell her.)
- *Three in ten girls* in the United States get pregnant at least once by age twenty.
- There are *seven hundred thousand teen pregnancies* every year.
- *Six in ten* pregnancies of women ages twenty to twenty-four are unplanned.
- *Half of all* pregnancies in the United States are unplanned, totaling almost three million every year.

Though you may prefer that your daughter's mom handle this topic, I trust I have relayed enough data to support *the importance of your leadership with your daughter on the subject of sex.*

Your Leadership Is Necessary

Here are a few guidelines to keep in mind before you have "the sex talk" with your daughter:

- Know that it will probably be uncomfortable at first (for both of you) so plan to *pace with her,* meaning that the *depth* and *length* of conversation will need to correspond with your daughter's age and comfort level.
- Ask more questions at first rather than give advice, remembering that the goal is to *dialogue not lecture.*
- Stand firm in knowing that during ongoing discussions, each of you will *increase your ability* to discuss this potentially awkward subject because you will already have started the conversation.
- *Ask your wife* (or a trusted, wise female friend) *for any insights* she believes would be important to share on sex from a woman's point of view.

Daughters Respect Fathers Who Stand for Something

Dr. Meg Meeker, author of *Strong Fathers, Strong Daughters*, encourages dads to give their daughters clear moral guidelines backed first by their own moral clarity, adding that "daughters respect fathers who stand for something. She wants to see conviction and leadership in her father...and needs to know your standards, because everyone else is trying to sell her theirs."

A lot more could be said on this topic, but I hope you are now motivated and willing to get the conversation started. I encourage you to take a moment to write out a couple of things you want to say so that you're ready once you take the initiative to talk with her about sex.

The two things I need to say to my daughter about sex are...

1.

2.

CHAPTER 37

THE SEX TALK: FAITH, CHOICE, AND VOICE

Now to the issue of faith and sex. A 2009 study by the National Campaign to Prevent Teen and Unplanned Pregnancy found that **80 percent** of unmarried *evangelical* young adults between the ages of eighteen and twenty-nine reported they had already had sex. This stands only in slight contrast to **88 percent** of all unmarried adults nationwide who said they were no longer virgins.

Why Christians Aren't Waiting Anymore

This data was published in a 2011 CNN article titled "Why Young Christians Aren't Waiting Anymore." The article highlights that Christians are saying "it's too hard to hold out" due to such factors as our sexualized and pleasure-oriented culture, coupled with the pervasiveness of pornography, which is constantly "only one click away" (underscoring the necessity of parents checking to see what their children are viewing on their electronic devices). If you factor in that men and women during biblical times probably married in their early teens, it makes sense why the increased temptations faced by those who get married later in life have led us to where we are today.

She Needs Things to Say Yes To

In an attempt to support faith communities, the National Campaign to Prevent Teen and Unplanned Pregnancy created in 2013 an online resource with practical tips parents can use to address this topic with their children. I resonate with their statement that **"teenagers [and young adults] need things to say 'yes' to, especially when we are asking them to say 'no' to pregnancy."** Add in that 57 percent of teen girls who had never had sex said that the main reason for their abstinence was that premarital sex went against their morals or religion, and it becomes evident that girls must define their moral convictions in order to navigate this issue strategically and wisely.

Help Her Explore Her Faith

Dad, can you see why it's so important for you to help your daughter say yes to her spiritual life? Help her explore her faith so she can clarify her sexual boundaries. Be her role model.

Encourage her to *write out* her stance on sex. You could draft a certificate (or search online for "free certificates for purity") that she signs to pledge her commitment to purity. Take her out for a special dinner and buy her a purity ring to commemorate the event. Celebrate her. Speak truth into her life. Be bold. Challenge her to think long term. She'll never forget it.

Now let's address the real possibility that your talk with her may be "too little too late." She may have already crossed lines, even her own boundaries, and is now struggling to process it all. And whether you want to believe that your little girl is messing around with guys, I can assure you there's a high likelihood that she is or has. I spend a fair amount of time talking through these issues with girls, and it's very common that they've gone farther than they planned to go and done things much earlier (both in terms of their age and the stage of the relationship) than they had planned to do. **The things done in secret that go against a girl's morals and values really do wreak havoc on her life.**

She Can't Undo Her Past but She Can Redirect Her Future

She must open up those areas where shame and guilt have taken root in order to receive love and healing truth en route to forgiveness (of the guy and of herself). Hard as it may be for your daughter to be honest with you, she needs a guy to give honest, tender, grace-filled input. You can lead her to truth about being her best self without compromise from this point forward. **The reality is that she can't undo the past, but she can redirect her future.**

A metaphor may help. Think of her mind as a refrigerator. If moldy food doesn't get removed, it will stink up the whole box. The only way to fix the problem is with light and air, coupled with removal of the rotten items. Dad, be her light and air, making sure to use gentleness in the process.

Urgent Need for Dads to Address This Issue

Bottom line: **There is an urgent need for dads to speak truth into their daughters' lives to counterbalance the norms our culture sets forth for kids about sex.**

> Recently a young woman told me it's "eating her up inside" that her Christian boyfriend isn't leading them both to stop when they're "close to the line." She told me she "feels way more guilty than he does." By contrast, she talked about a guy she dated last year who

was very clear about boundaries. "I felt more loved by his abstaining because in essence he was saying, 'I care more about your spirit and heart than about the fun of wanting to make out with you.'" Then she added, "I don't think guys put the two together."

When a girl thinks a guy is with her only because of what she will do sexually, it messes with her head and heart because she ends up believing that *who she is* isn't enough to keep him interested. Of course she never believes this at first when it feels good and she's on an emotional high. But I'm talking about after she comes down off the high and crashes emotionally. It's then that she feels she's not valued for her mind or heart but only for her body. This is devastating to girls in the end.

Here are some things I hear from girls and young women:

What I Hear from Girls About Sex

"Oral sex isn't sex." (That's when I love to ask, "How can it not be sex when the second half of the phrase is *sex*?")

"I only do it because I know he likes it even though I think it's gross and actually hate it."

"After I do things with guys, I don't feel good about myself because that's when the guilt sets in."

"It's hard to stop doing things once he expects it even if I'm not into it anymore."

"I'd rather just cuddle, but if I don't give him what he wants, he'll dump me or tell all his friends I'm a prude."

Blunt as this may be, here is what I tell girls about oral sex: "When you are down on all fours, doing things that make you feel dirty, disgusting, maybe even guilty, you are not in the position God wants you to be in. Stand up and look that boy in the eyes. You are his equal and shouldn't being doing anything you don't want to do that makes you feel yucky."

Sadly though, girls often receive the message through sexual exploration with guys that it's okay to be *used, forced, manipulated, demeaned, diminished, taken advantage of, and even pushed to do things that don't feel right.*

Stifled and Submerged Voices

Don't get me wrong. I know it takes two to tango. We all know that many women lure and use men as much as men use women. Yet regardless of who is enticing whom, my heart hurts for these girls because they often don't believe they can say no. Often their voice is *stifled and submerged,* and sometimes it takes a long while for them to acknowledge that they don't want to do what they're doing, but they're caught in a cycle of pleasing the guy at any cost to themselves. And because girls don't always *honestly* talk about or admit the painful side of it all, the myth about it being wonderful and perfect is perpetuated.

One of the most heartbreaking realities I often hear is that girls who get caught in this crazy-making cycle stop ***making a choice and using their voice.*** These two themes, *choice* and *voice*, are key words I repeat regularly when teaching girls how to become empowered. (Feel free to use them in your dialogue with your daughter. You don't need to tell her where you heard it!) I tell her that if she wants to grow to be an empowered woman, she has to activate *both* of these things. They go hand in hand and are absolutely necessary on the pathway to becoming a strong, assertive, bold, confidant woman. *And the only way to acquire these skills is to practice using them.*

Teach Her to Say No (Even If It's to You)

If you truly want your daughter to learn to make choices while using her voice, then you have to allow her to practice these things with you. Not easy, I know. I understand that fathers want their daughters to be respectful and obedient...*all the time.* But if you embrace the bigger picture, you will be willing to let her push back while learning to assert herself in the process of finding her own voice.

The time is now for you to help your daughter:

- Set sexual boundaries.
- Learn to say no (even to you at times).
- Figure out what to say yes to.
- Stand up for herself even if she's the only one standing.
- Make a choice and use (or sometimes find) her voice.

If It's Science You Want

To increase your knowledge, I highly recommend the 2008 groundbreaking book *Hooked: New Science on How Casual Sex Is Affecting Our Children.* Written by two medical doctors, Joe McIlhaney Jr. and Freda

McKissic Bush, the book presents scientific facts about the way sexual activity affects the brain. For example, the neurotransmitter dopamine (the pleasure center) rewards the brain for both positive and negative risk-taking behavior, with sex being one of the strongest generators of this chemical. Another neurochemical that is released during sex is oxytocin (which is active in both genders but primarily in females), leading to a feeling of attachment that isn't necessarily accurate or real. These authors note that "young women especially need to be aware of the powerful bonding effect of oxytocin" because breaking these bonds when a relationship ends not only can cause depression but also can make it harder to bond with someone else down the road. After reading this book, you will be better equipped to pass along to your daughter important facts that will increase her self-awareness.

Be bold, dad. **Tell your daughter what you believe about sex, remembering that your words will impact her even if she doesn't tell you they do.** As one teenager said to me, "I don't care as much if my mom knows about what I've done with guys. But there's nothing worse than knowing I've disappointed my dad."

Be Bold. If You Don't Talk, Others Will.

If you don't know where to begin this conversation, you can follow the advice of teens in one study who said the best way to open up dialogue with adults is to simply *talk* about what they see in the media regarding sex, relationships, and love (or lust).

Here is what you can do: Buy two or three current magazines that have words on the cover about sex, sexuality, and body image. Bring them on your date with your daughter and look together at the messages being promoted. (I guarantee this will be a big eye-opener for you.) Then talk about how her faith differs or lines up with what the magazine endorses. **Remember to ask questions, not just lecture.**

PART FOUR

Under the Foundation: Looking Deeper at Yourself

CHAPTER 38

THE FATHER WOUND OF ANGER

If you were to ask, *"Michelle, what one piece of advice could you give me about where to focus my attention so that I can be the best dad I can be?"* without hesitation I would answer, **"Stop venting your anger at your daughter."**

- Your anger destroys her spirit.
- Your anger shuts her down.
- Your anger makes her give up and stop trying.
- Your anger makes her believe that she is unlovable, unworthy, and not worth loving.
- Your anger crushes the core of who she is.

I hear more stories from girls on how their dads' anger deeply impacts them than I do on anything else about their dads. I see the pain in their eyes as they tell me the stories, and my heart breaks because I believe their dads love them. Yet oftentimes when dad has had one too many things go wrong in his day, he comes home and his daughter gets his fumes. It doesn't take much for him then to blow, often treating her in a way that he later regrets. But by then the damage is done and she is left bleeding on the inside.

Listen to twenty-eight-year-old Angie's story:

Angie's Story

I'm sitting here avoiding the topic of father wounds. I have so many other things to distract me that it's not even funny, especially when I don't like going to these hard places. So I don't even know where to start. Maybe naming the injuries I feel are the most important, in that they have impacted my life the most, is a good place to begin.

It's as hard to place blame on my dad as it is to realize how much he has really hurt me. So here goes naming injury #1: Reacting in anger.

My dad has never been very good at expressing himself, so he has always let things bottle up until they reach a boiling point. He can go from a three to ten very fast. I know that I have talked in counseling about his way of reacting to things as being "his stuff," but I still feel like I am subconsciously always avoiding this explosion—walking on eggshells.

This can lead me to be passive-aggressive, and not only to him but to my mom who also gets some of the blame for letting Dad be the way he is. But then I take it out on myself through my eating disorder.

I have always felt the heaviness of my dad's depression too, which can be just as bad as his explosions, and probably more common. I can smell it in the air and I feel it deep in the air. And I feel it deep inside me. Yet as much as my dad and I have not connected and understood each other, I have been deeply connected to his emotional aura for as far back as I can remember.

Dad, I know you are human and there's no way you can ever completely avoid hurting your daughter. But my goal here is to make you *more aware* of your impact on her by your emotional reactions. Did you hear how Angie internalized her dad's anger, only then to have it manifest through an eating disorder as her way of taking it out on herself? And though her dad is not completely to blame, a daughter can easily view a dad's upset as being her fault.

Think Fragile Flower

Think back to the day your daughter was born and you saw her as a fragile flower. Recall how gently you held her, careful not to break her, taking extra precautions so as not to move too aggressively or let her head drop. You made sure not to shout or talk too loud in order not to scare her. *Do you remember that indescribable feeling when you were in awe of her adorable little features while thinking that you had never held anything so small or so beautiful in all your life?*

Your Valuable Treasure

This is how you still need to think of holding her, even when she pushes every button in you and is extremely hard to love, or even like, on some days. She is still delicate on the inside and needs to be handled with kid gloves. Treat her like **the most valuable treasure** that she truly is.

One key thing my dad has had to do with me is to soften his tone in order to connect with me. I am innately wired to be very sensitive, which is a gift when it comes to my role as a counselor but isn't always convenient in dad-daughter interactions. I know this doesn't come naturally for him—or any man for that matter—but it can be done.

And just in case the word *soft* makes you feel less than a man, it may help to recall that God Himself said in Proverbs 15:1 (NLT) that "a gentle [soft] answer deflects anger, but harsh words make tempers flare." So I suppose that if God the Father is giving this challenge, then it must be manly to use softness to turn away from blowing our top.

Look into Her Eyes

I believe that a dad can change his anger patterns by truly looking the one he loves in the eyes. I'm not expecting you to be superhuman, but I do want to challenge you today to make a covenant with your mouth to not vent anger at your daughter from this day forward. **Choose today to set a new course by determining that when triggered, you will walk away and get your feet back on the ground before responding.** No more harshness.

(Think of it this way: If you were offered a million dollars to stop being harsh for a day, week, or month, you would be motivated to do it, right? Your daughter is your million-dollar investment.)

An Obstructed View

We've all heard the term *blind spot*, that area where a person's view is obstructed, when it comes to driving. I think this expression relates to life beyond the wheel. The way you "drive" (react) with your daughter in your "car" (life/relationship) impacts every part of her life because she's along for the ride, for good or bad.

I know it can be hard sometimes for any of us to come out from under the illusion that we're an expert driver, especially when it means admitting that we didn't see something on the road. And to make matters a bit more complicated for you, dad, think about what happens when someone else (especially your wife) points out something you missed when you were behind the wheel. That's usually when the walls of defensiveness go up and conflict is activated.

Okay, maybe if we lived in isolation we would have the freedom to "drive" any way we want. But when we live in close proximity to others, and especially when one of those riding in the "car" is your daughter, then you truly don't have the freedom to "drive" any way you want. After all, there are rules of the road. And every move you make as a driver impacts the lives of those in the car.

We've all seen the words inscribed on our sideview mirrors: *Objects in mirror are closer than they appear.* How true those words are in relation to your daughter. **Whether she's in the backseat of your "car" or in a "car" following behind you,** she is right there watching, listening, and copying you. I'd say that's 24-7 driver's education at its best…or worst.

With this theme of father wounds, I trust that this driving illustration serves as a reminder that your daughter is impacted daily by your driving, particularly in the area of your blind spots.

Your Driving Habits Lead the Way for Her

Your driving habits lead the way for her. Take note of the times you make excuses for how you drive or the times you feel justified in the way you drive when she's in your car. *Do you tell yourself that it's okay if you blow up since you're the parent, but come down hard on her for doing the same thing?*

It's only when we admit we are human and in need of help that we can change. It's then that we're open to seeing the areas where our view is obstructed. Model that kind of openness to your daughter with the words of James 1:19 (MSG) guiding you to "lead with your ears, follow up with your tongue, and let anger straggle along in the rear."

Ask her for feedback on how you're doing with the anger issue. Be open to hearing about how your driving is affecting her. There's no better time than the present to improve your driving record.

The area where I know I am hurting my daughter the most is...

I close this chapter with a story that ends with a positive challenge. My friend Nancy recently attended a conference that finished on the evening before Father's Day. The main speaker that last night, Cal Pierce, asked people to stand up if they had never received a blessing from their father. Most of the room stood up. Tears flowed readily. He then told the group that *almost everywhere he goes, about 70 percent of the room stands up when he asks that question.* Shocking really. Sad statistic.

Dad, you have an opportunity to change these statistical norms by daily blessing your daughter. Your anger responses will turn around if you choose proactively to bless her instead.

The blessing I will speak into my daughter's life today is...

CHAPTER 39

GETTING UNDER THE ANGER

"Just wait 'til your father gets home." I'm sure you heard these words a time or two back when you were a kid. You may even be activating some traumatic memory just by hearing them again now.

These seven words don't always put you dads in the best light, do they? They really do give you a difficult setup before you even walk in the door. But the positive part is noteworthy and validating: **Your male strength is crucial to help maintain balance in your home. You, dad, are important and you are needed.**

Anger Squelches Her Spirit

Let me ask you a question: What primary emotion *(happy, sad, angry, scared, confused)* does this statement suggest will be on your face when you, dear father, get home? My guess: *anger*. As I stated in the previous chapter, I believe anger is the number one way most fathers lose (or wound) their daughters. Uncontrolled anger from a dad squelches and can even destroy his daughter's spirit.

Let me clarify. Go back to the five primary emotions cited above and ask yourself which emotion would be activated if the following were to happen between you and your daughter:

- She doesn't clean her room after being asked.
- She disrespects her mom (or you).
- She teases (bullies or persecutes) her siblings.
- She has a meltdown and slams the door.
- Her monthly phone usage is double her plan allotment.
- She leaves her cell phone in her locker on Friday and then demands (not asks) that you get it.

- You drop what you're doing to fix something of hers that is broken, but the only feedback you get from her is negative.
- She gets angry while doing her chemistry or math homework, which prompts you, "the fixer," to try to help. But she rejects your help, saying (or screaming) that you're making it worse.
- She brings a boy home for the first time, and you inadvertently say something she finds embarrassing, which results in her shunning you for the rest of the evening.

Now tally your score. What percentage of your responses were in the *anger category* and what percentage were in the *happy, sad, scared,* or *confused categories*? My guess is that anger again won out.

The Anger Funnel

Is it possible that some of your underlying emotions are being denied (hurt, sadness, fear, helplessness) and those emotions are instead coming out through the anger funnel?

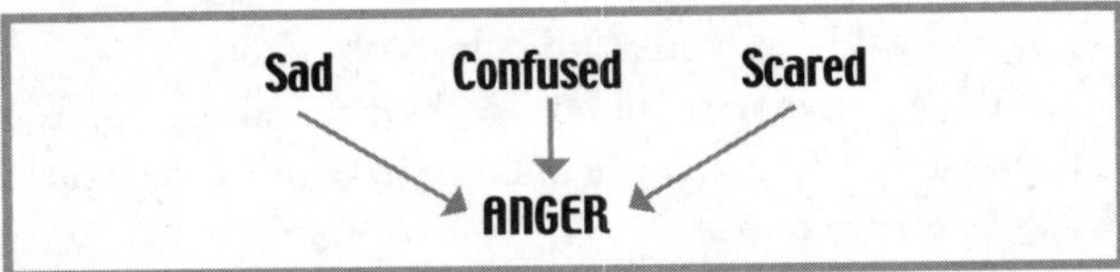

It would make sense that if you were doing your best to help your daughter with her homework, and she rejects your help and instead criticizes you, a legitimate response would be sadness ("being hurt" is in the *sad* category).

But sadness is often viewed by men as a weak emotion. So instead of admitting the sadness, it can be easy to opt for a seemingly stronger emotion of anger. (I use the word *seemingly* because although anger packs a punch and presents as intense, it creates an adrenaline surge, resulting in less clarity and less control rather than more strength.)

Damage Control After Dad's Anger

Though this chapter may seem like a mini therapy session, I'm telling you this because anger is where so many girls carry the most hurt from their dads. And because this book is aimed at helping you understand what your daughter *really* wants from you, **I want you to look underneath your anger so you can uproot it.**

But first, here are some honest responses from girls between the ages of thirteen and thirty when I asked them the following questions:

- From your point of view, what makes your dad angry?
- Is that anger ever about you?
- What do you feel inside when your dad gets angry or frustrated with you?

Heart-Wrenching Responses from Girls About Dad's Anger

"It really depends on the day when it comes to what makes my dad angry. But he gets really upset if he thinks we don't appreciate all that he and my mom do for us kids. And lying and disrespectfulness."

"I make my dad angry. Just the act of me breathing makes him angry. I am the source of his anger, and he has mentioned that I am on a few occasions. When my father gets frustrated with me, I really let him have it—the cold shoulder, that is."

"What makes my dad angry is when people aren't honest. He is very honest, and when asked, he says he values that in others. **My dad really doesn't like it when I am annoying."**

"When people disrespect him. He actually hardly ever gets mad at me. And if he is, it's more just me feeling like it's anger, but really it's just him telling me I need to do something or change something."

"My dad gets angry when he is concerned or worried. **If his anger is directed at me, it makes me feel like I have disappointed him.** I feel like I have done something wrong, and it makes me feel sad."

"When work is stressful and isn't going well. My attitude angers him most of the time too. I don't really care."

"I think that my dad's own mistakes and guilt make him angry. I don't know if any of that anger is about me and I don't really care."

"If my dad gets frustrated with me for a legitimate reason, then I feel like I deserve it and I listen to him and act accordingly. But if he misdirects his anger or frustration on me (which he frequently does), then I get *really* ticked and tell him off. At the same time **it hurts my feelings, but I don't tell him that."**

"My dad is very even-tempered. It takes a lot to make him mad. He gets angry when I say things without thinking first. I say how I feel. I don't think Dad gets angry at me as much as it's disappointment."

Are you catching the underlying themes in these statements? What I hear every one of these girls saying is that she knows her dad is human, but when he demands respect without modeling it, her emotional walls go up and she disengages. And though a couple of them said, "I don't care," I can tell you that I don't buy it. All girls care. It's how we're wired. **Never believe us when we say we don't care.**

You, Dad, Set the Tone

I talked earlier about being a *gentle* pursuer of her heart. And one way to measure yourself in this area is by your *tone of voice*. Some dads have told me they're sick of the "soft approach" with their rebellious or angry daughters, but *if you come at her with aggression, then you'll get the same thing back.* **You have to treat her the way you want to be treated.** If you want respect, you have to give it. Don't use her freak out as validation for your anger response. **You set the tone in your home.**

Love Ranks Above Respect on Venus

I know it's hard to have a calm response to an overly reactive daughter because everything in you shouts that she isn't respecting you (or someone else, especially when it's her mom). You as a man live with the "respect code" as the most important of all virtues. Yet I'm here to tell you that *on Venus we put love far above respect* (just ask Emerson Eggerichs, author of *Love and Respect*). You can't fight fire with fire. You know that. Now you have to live it.

When a daughter melts down over something in her world that isn't working right, most of the time she isn't thinking about being disrespectful or dishonoring. Instead, she's feeling intense emotion and *needs your help to regroup and reground.* She needs gentle love and support from you, not anger, to come through it.

Don't React to Her Reaction

This, in essence, means you have to work very hard at not reacting to her reaction. You have to respond first in the way you want to see her respond. *Give yourself time to calm down first. Then come back and talk things out or give discipline.*

After all, God had a reason for saying, "Fathers, don't exasperate your children by coming down hard on them. Take them by the hand and lead them in the way of the Master" (Ephesians 6:4 MSG).

Your soft response is the quickest way to diffuse her fire.

Your harsh response is the quickest way to pour fuel on her fire.

Because controlling your anger is paramount to moving forward positively with your daughter, I invite you to answer these two questions:

The thing that most easily pushes my anger button with my daughter is...

My proactive plan so that I respond from here on out with love and gentleness when she pushes my anger button is...

PS: One strategy to change the anger dance may be to go back to your answer in chapter 6 ("Thinking Backward") regarding that *one thing* you want your daughter to say about you at the end of your life. Then when your anger button is pushed, *if you focus instead on that one thing that really matters in the end*, it may help you to stay grounded in the present while being less reactive.

CHAPTER 40

TAKE AN INVENTORY: AS A DAD, WITH YOUR DAD

My best friend of more than thirty-five years, Connie Patty, lives in the Czech Republic where she and her husband, Dave, lead a missions organization with ministries in twelve Eastern European countries. Dave is a phenomenal teacher, and not only has he been teaching on the fatherhood of God for the past few years, but he has also developed a paradigm to explain three main ways a father impacts his children: *wounds, voids,* and *gifts.*

Using his model as a foundation, I will share some ideas you can use to assess your relationship with your daughter in light of the way your relationship with your father has affected you.

What a Dad Does That Hurts

First, father wounds are specific things a dad *does* that hurt his child—physical, verbal, sexual, spiritual, or emotional wounding. Dr. Jim Friesen calls this "B Trauma" to represent the bad things that happen to a person. A momentous incident between my dad and me definitely falls into this category.

Another Story About My Dad and Me

At the age of twenty-four I was living at home after college while working as a dental assistant, a job I didn't really like. I was also doing volunteer youth ministry at the church where my dad pastored. This was also a season when I was in a lot of emotional distress and expressing a lot of anger. At the time, I had no idea where it came from or why it was there, but my poor family got the brunt of it.

One evening I remember working on a craft project where everything that could go wrong did go wrong despite my asking God for His help.

> And it didn't take long for me to conclude that I must not rank high enough on His priority list for Him to show up for me.
>
> I didn't hesitate to express my frustration out loud, which didn't go over so well. In my dad's book, this was paramount to an unpardonable sin. When he heard me vent my anger at God, he turned to me and said sharply, "Michelle, God ought to strike you dead." Yikes. That wound really stung. For a long time.
>
> My dad and I revisit this story from time to time. A couple of years ago I reminded him that until I got into counseling where God cleaned that wound, I honestly thought that God really would strike me dead if I were "too this" or "too that." I then asked him where he thought I got that punitive message about God.
>
> "Probably from me," he said.
>
> His backstory (which I only now know) was that being raised Catholic, he was trained to believe that if he ever walked into the door of a Protestant church, God would strike him dead. So without a second thought at the time of my craft-project meltdown, he passed the same message on to me. That's how wounds seem to work, don't they?

What a Dad Doesn't Do That Hurts

Second, father voids are things a dad *does not do* that hurt his child—broken promises, unkept commitments, lack of time, negligence, and no-to-low investment financially, emotionally, spiritually, mentally, and relationally. This can be called "A Trauma" or the absence of good things.

Voids are defined as the absence of necessary investments. "A Trauma" is much harder to see, acknowledge, or even validate since there isn't something tangible to show for it. Yet oftentimes "A Trauma" is harder to heal from than "B Trauma" because of the way these deficits affect trust and attachment.

Some of you may resonate more with the description of *vacuums* rather than voids if you had a dad who "sucked life out of you." This could have happened verbally with criticisms or comparisons, or relationally if he showed favoritism and preferential treatment to one sibling over another, or physically and emotionally if he invested in his own self-serving interests rather than your needs.

Whether you have father *wounds* or *voids*, there is hurt and damage either way. And despite differing levels of intensity, all of it is substantial and potentially devastating. *Until healing happens.*

Dr. Ken Canfield, in *The Heart of the Father,* ties this all together: "Many fathers feel inadequate for fathering. They lack confidence, so they hand the child back to their wife. The first thing that such hesitant fathers must do is process their past. There is a direct and powerful connection between fathering of the past and fathering of the present."

What a Dad Does to Heal and Invest

Third, father gifts are things a dad *does to invest* in his children, to let them know in *word and action* that they are valuable, worthy, special, treasured, loved, adored, and respected.

Despite receiving *wounds, voids,* or *gifts* from our earthly father, we're all in need of filling from our Abba Father. In *The Quest for Authentic Manhood,* Dr. Robert Lewis writes:

Pain Tied to Our Fathers... or Lost Dreams

> Underneath the surface of men's lives there's a lot of pain they haven't resolved and they don't know how to talk about it. Men look at the guys around them and those guys look like they're doing all right. They look like they have it all together. But underneath there's pain.
>
> Some of that pain relates to their dads and unresolved issues there. Some of it relates to dreams, things that never came to fruition. Some of it relates to failures, places where they've messed up and don't know how to fix it.
>
> It's interesting that in an age where technology is up, intimacy is down. Men know people but people don't know them. Men in particular are lonely. No one has access to their lives and they're not sure how to get out and get connected.

I agree that men in general long to be known yet are conditioned to hide behind a tough exterior. Factor in societal norms that perpetuate the stereotype that men are supposed to be strong and that it's not masculine for a guy to "be in touch with his feelings." The result? Men often push down or ignore the realities of what they're really feeling and thinking, especially in areas of their wounds, and they numb out with sports, television, addictions (alcohol, porn, work, exercise), all the while living lives of emotional starvation.

Choose Not to Hide Anymore

Don't hide any longer behind your pain, hurts, work, busyness, or__________(fill in the blank). **Your daughter needs you to be whole and alive and emotionally healthy in order to invest well in her heart needs.**

We've all heard it said that a chain is only as strong as its weakest link. I've discovered that we're only strong emotionally, spiritually, mentally, physically, and even interpersonally in direct proportion to the healing we've experienced for our internal wounds. Our wounds are our weakest links. *Unhealed wounds weaken us.*

Our Wounds Weaken Us

It's from our wounds that we hit an 8, 9, or 10 on a 0-to-10 scale of intensity when we forcefully react rather than respond. That's how we know it's old pain and not the current scenario that's driving the reaction. *This is where healing must happen in order for us to be healthy.*

Here is how I explain this to my clients:

On a 0-to-10 scale, with 10 being the highest intensity and 0 being neutral or calm, if you quickly hit an 8, 9, or 10 in a situation, it's *always* your "old stuff." The current situation flips on the switch, but the hard wiring was there long before the event. This is often why those who are interacting with the person who is having the reaction are confused. The reaction confirms that it doesn't fully tie to the present and has a clear link to a past experience.

A product on the market called Wound-Be-Gone claims to dramatically accelerate wound healing. *Wouldn't it be great if there were a magic potion (a quick fix) that could instantly heal an emotional wound?*

The only wound-be-gone formula I know is:

Four-Step Process to Healing

1. **H**onestly face the hurt ("you've got to feel to heal").
2. **E**xpress the pain (safe verbal and emotional release of what's inside).
3. **A**llow another to walk with you (a safe witness to your pain).
4. **L**et go of the pain (forgive).

You might honestly think you don't have any issues or unresolved pain from your past. You could be right. But just in case there are areas where you are unknowingly (or knowingly) hurting your daughter from the overflow of some high-intensity wounds, I want to suggest one practical way to help increase your process of self-discovery. Ask your daughter (or wife) if she sees any area in your life where you have a wound. I'm not asking your daughter to be your therapist; instead, I'm inviting you to talk with her about where your intensity is impacting her. Sometimes a woman's intuition can help guide you if you are open to her input. Then be willing to see a counselor for even a few sessions (if long-term therapy isn't your style).

Healing is possible, but it takes work.

Now is the time to look underneath the hood and examine the engine. Probe deeper out of love for your daughter. Now is the time to heal…for your sake and your daughter's sake.

1. **A father *wound* I carry is...**

2. **A father *void* I have is...**

3. **A father *gift* I've received is...**

CHAPTER 41

HEALING YOUR OWN FATHER WOUNDS

To heal as an adult from wounds that your father inflicted some twenty, thirty, or even forty years ago may seem like an impossibility or perhaps an exercise in futility. Maybe you've thought, *Why dredge up the past? There's nothing I can do about it now anyway, so why talk about it?*

Let me ask you this: Do you have any sports injuries from junior high, high school, or college? I imagine it's the rare man who has escaped without evidence of surviving a blow of some kind to his body. Do you ever still experience discomfort as a result of those old injuries? Most likely you answered yes.

We all are impacted by physical injuries from our past, whether we admit they are there or not. Ignoring them or choosing not to talk about them doesn't make them go away. If they're there, they're there.

It's the same with emotional injuries. These are the places where we once were hurt, but perhaps we've long since tried to ignore, forget, or minimize.

I am not one of those therapists who encourages people to stay a victim, to not take responsibility or accountability for their actions, or to blame everyone else for their problems. In fact, it's quite the opposite.

Healing Comes When the Injury Is Opened

I believe that healing is possible only when we open up what's inside and face it honestly. It is then that the infection can be cleaned out so that health can result. And when it comes to emotional injuries, healing isn't just a cognitive process. It is one where emotionally stored pain has to be emotionally faced and emotionally felt so that it can be released. Like the adage says, *What you don't feel can't heal.*

I also believe that I can't take people farther than where I've gone in my own healing journey. I'd like to share some of that with you.

Opening Up About My Grandfather Wound

I spent eight years in my own grueling counseling process. That journey led me to later pursue this field as a profession because I wanted to help others experience freedom as I had. I do have father wounds in my history, some from my dad as a result of him projecting onto me his beliefs that didn't always fully resonate with me, but more significantly from my grandfather.

My grandfather was "a man of the cloth" as well as a farmer. He was known as an upstanding citizen in his southwestern Minnesota town of three thousand, as well as the host of "Morning Meditations Bible Program," which was broadcast from his rural farmhouse. He sought hard to maintain his stellar image, but behind closed doors he also was an abuser. He died when I was eight years old, so thankfully his sexual abuse came to an end. But make no mistake, what he did to me not only left huge scars mentally, emotionally, and spiritually, but it lived on inside me for years after his death. This is what led me to counseling.

Had it not been for the intense healing process I went through, I wouldn't know Jesus or Abba Father God the way I do now and I wouldn't be able to sit in the intensity of the counseling work I do either. For those reasons, among many, I now can honestly say that I do believe Romans 8:28, "that in all things God works for the good of those who love him, who have been called according to his purpose."

My wounds were loud and clear—to me and to my family, that is. You see, when it comes to heart wounds, they tend to speak louder than most anything else. As I think back to my first thirty years of life, I loved God, had lots of friends, obeyed my parents, went to church, and was a good girl. But on the inside I had extreme fears, intense self-loathing, unexplained guilt, severe overreactions, a long-standing eating disorder, and on it goes. Yet most of this was my own private pain. Most never knew.

Facing My Pain Was the Hardest Thing I've Ever Done

I can tell you without qualification that facing my pain was the hardest thing I've ever done. To walk into my counselor's office week after week and not know what would emerge was terrifying. But I can also tell you that it was through this process that all the head knowledge I learned in Bible school finally made its way down to my hurting heart. I did feel and I did heal. And like my heart friend Paul Young says, "God must really like process because everyone I know is in one."

Here is a little bit of what that process looked like for me. As memories of my abuse would emerge, each week my counselor would ask Jesus to show me where He was in the memory picture. And time and again, I would see Him. I had to learn to look and listen because this was all new to me at the time.

Jesus Was There with Me

I'll never forget the day *I saw Him crying* over what was being done to me. **It was life-changing to know Jesus was there with me and felt my pain.** I had to work through the question of why He didn't stop it, but in time I came to understand that because God gives free will, some choose to commit evil acts that violate the core of who He created them to be.

I Want to Exalt the Healer, Not My Story

Some may think I'm loony tunes to have interacted with Jesus like this. Some may believe I fabricated it just to make myself feel better. I beg to differ. I'm not that smart or clever. All I can tell you is that *I once was blind and now I see.* I am not the same as I once was. Fear no longer grips me. Self-loathing is gone. My eating disorder is healed. And on it goes. Jesus was real to me then and He's real to me now. *I tell you this not to exalt my story but to exalt my Healer.*

I ask myself if it was worth it to open up my grandfather wounds. Absolutely. *It's the only way that the lies and the pain could have been released in exchange for truth.* I would go through the process again to know Jesus as I do now. And the only thing that trumps the volume or intensity of woundedness is *joy*.

Returning to Joy

Dr. Jim Friesen says that joy is the most powerful emotion we can have and a "return to joy" is the goal of healing. And though I've had more than one client ask how someone can return to joy when it's never been there in the first place, I have to believe that because joy is something God places inside each of us at birth, it is He who can reignite it in all of us.

The problem for some, however, is that there is no conscious memory of joy ever being there. Maybe that's you. It's important to know that **the goal is not only to get through the pain to find the joy underneath, but to have truth replace the lies that have been attached to the unhealed wounds.**

In *Mothering Ourselves: Help and Healing for Adult Daughters,* Dr. Evelyn Bassoff says that whether our wounds were from our mother or our father, there comes a time when we must engage in a healing process in order to move on. Here is an adapted version of her 8-Step Healing Model that she describes as "complicated" but that also offers a pathway to "true healing":

8-Step Healing Model

1. Recognize that our father has wounded us.
2. Understand the nature of those wounds.
3. Express our legitimate hurt or outrage.
4. Find ways to soothe our pain in a healthy way.
5. Find creative ways to transform our pain.
6. Try not to repeat old destructive patterns.
7. Extend empathy to the wounding father (if abuse took place, this step is potentially impossible and that is appropriate).
8. Try to restructure the present father-adult child relationship.

The two pieces I would add to this list are:

My Additions to the Healing Process

1. Invite Jesus and Abba Father God to bring their truth to the wounded places.
2. Open up to rebuilding or reworking a healthy relationship with God to replace the lies and wounds from an earthly dad.

This model encourages honesty toward past hurts. The hurts need to be called for what they were and are—not exaggerated or minimized. This is often a challenging first step.

Don't hesitate to call on your wife, a close friend, a pastor, or a counselor to be a mirror and listening ear to your story, a story that you may have disconnected from years ago. Let that person validate your pain, even if it's uncomfortable for you to open up the wound and feel your feelings.

It's Worth It to Look Within

The pathway to healing is never an easy one, but it is so worth it. I know this from personal experience. And I would never trade my healing journey for anything in the world because once I turned around and faced those dreaded monsters from my past that I often felt were looking over my shoulder, I was able then to live with more freedom, more capacity to connect with others in deeper ways, and greater ability to take risks. Overall, life is a lot more fun now that energy flows with less effort.

For the sake of your daughter, you've got to do it. You'll be able to love her better once your wounds are cleaned out and healed. She's worth it. You're worth it.

She's Worth It. You're Worth It.

These questions below are intended to help you to look within yourself:

Three adjectives to describe how my dad made me feel are...

1.

2.

3.

Three adjectives to describe how I make my daughter feel are...

1.

2.

3.

Where I typically hit an 8, 9, or 10 in emotional intensity is...

Where I know I could use some healing for my own stuff is...

CHAPTER 42

HOW TO REBUILD THE BRIDGE

I've spoken with many dads who admit they've had a significant role in destroying the bridge between themselves and their daughters. I want you to hear that I'm not standing in judgment of you for the past, but I am challenging you to take the bull by the horns and make amends *today.*

Start Rebuilding Today

You'll recall me saying that men would rather do nothing than do it wrong. This applies to making amends too. Perhaps you've held off crossing the bridge to her heart because you think too much time has passed or she'll never talk to you again because of an offense. This is where you'll have to be wise moving forward. I'd suggest starting with a letter if she's not okay with seeing you or doesn't feel safe with you. Perhaps texting is all she can handle right now.

But no matter the path you choose (or are forced to choose if she has closed the door), you'll have to honor her boundaries and track with her level of comfort in the potential rebuilding process.

And never underestimate the power of prayer. She may not be okay with you talking to her today or tomorrow, but you can always talk to God today and tomorrow. Write out a list of things you will commit to praying for *daily* until you have answers from Abba Father God. Ask for miracles so that your daughter's heart (and yours) can heal.

There's Power in Prayer

My prayer request in relationship to my daughter is...

My prayer request for me in all of this is...

I know a dad who struggled with his daughter for years, and then one day she announced that she was joining the military. He wondered how she would do (but never told her) and he committed to *pray daily* for healing in her life. **He opted to use his voice vertically rather than horizontally since she didn't have ears to hear him anyway.** You can imagine his surprise when she invited him to pin her at graduation, prompting him to send me a picture of them and this note:

A Grateful Dad's Story

The road was a bittersweet journey, with ups and downs, even after I learned a few things about teenage girls from you. I know that this moment does not mean the end of my relationship struggles with my daughter, but it is a pretty good image depicting an intact relationship between a young woman heading out in a right direction and an old battered dad who still apparently means a lot to her.

Lay Down Your Weapons

Another key piece of the rebuilding process (if this is where you're at with your daughter) is to **lay your weapons down.** You can't approach her with defensiveness or in "attack mode" if you want to repair the bridge.

If you care *more* about her hurt and her heart than you do about your position and being right, then here are some guidelines for rebuilding the bridge to her heart:

Rebuilding the Bridge to Her Heart

- **Ask questions with a sincere desire to know the answer.**

  "I know I hurt you with my words yesterday. When you came to me I didn't listen well. You were right about that piece. I want to listen now. Can you please tell me again what you want me to hear?"

- **Ask forgiveness for specifics, not generalities.**

  "Last night I was tired after work and took it out on you. I saw the look of hurt in your eyes when I got angry, yet I chose not to meet you in the way you needed me to. Will you please forgive me?"

- **Never mix amends with criticism (subtle or direct).**

  "I know I was harsh, but so were you. If you want to tell me now what you were saying last night, I will try to listen. But you need to meet me halfway and not be as emotional this time around."

I'm sure it goes without saying that this last tactic will bomb and is an example of what *not* to say. **The key is to picture her heart in yours and proceed with caution.**

One way to think about the impact your words have on your daughter is to visualize what a plant looks like in the heat of summer when it hasn't been watered for a few days. A while back I bought four luscious rhododendron plants and set them by my back porch for a week before planting them. I checked daily at first to make sure they were getting enough water, but when we got a good douse of Oregon rain, I figured they were good so I stopped checking. When I went to plant them that next weekend, the poor things looked as if they were dead. It shocked me that in just two or three days, the soil had dried up and they looked like they weren't going to make it.

She Can Wilt Fast

Similarly, your daughter is like those plants. *With the intensity of the environmental conditions around her, she can fade fast when she isn't being watered with words of kindness, affirmation, encouragement, support, and validation.*

She needs you to *consistently* water her with your words of love, blessing, and affirmation. She needs you to speak into her life and pour *refreshing words*—words that inspire and awaken her to thrive and flourish—into the soil of her heart so she can withstand the conditions around her. She needs *lots* and *lots* and *lots* of watering. This is a key factor to seeing your daughter bloom.

Sometimes, depending on the severity of the offense from a dad to his daughter (sexual, verbal, physical, or spiritual abuse, for example), you may have to live with the bridge the way it is for now or perhaps forever. What I do know is that any demands on your part will backfire, especially if there has ever been any misuse of power between you.

She Will Set the Rebuilding Pace

It's your daughter who will set the rebuilding pace. And if she's got the "stop sign" on her life and heart held up toward you, your best options are to:

- Do your own work. Find a mentor, pastor, or counselor to help you work through all that is being activated and stirred up in you.
- Pray for her and for yourself; be specific.
- Write letters to her (that you may or may not give her) that let *you* connect with *your* heart.

Before we leave this topic of bridge building, and whether or not your relationship needs repair, write out a prayer or a wish that you have for your daughter.

Dear God, You say that I do not have because I do not ask (James 4:2), so I am coming to You as a Father, asking You to move in my daughter's heart and life by doing the following...

CHAPTER 43

BUILDING A LEGACY

Earlier we talked about how sticks and stones, when thrown, really do hurt, especially when they are words being hurled. But now I want to give you a different and compelling way to think about rocks.

Every man I've ever known has played with stones at some time during his childhood. I'm guessing you did too. To state the obvious, here are some things that can be done with rocks:

Uses for Stones

1. Throw them. (Of course this is the number one answer I hear from men when I ask them this question.)
2. Skip them (across water).
3. Construct something with them.

But the thing that usually isn't mentioned, though it's very significant since God brought it up as something for fathers to do, is:

Build a Monument

4. Build a monument.

This last point comes from Joshua 4 when God led the Israelites to cross the Jordan River as He held back the water until all of them passed through the riverbed. Let's pick up the story with God's instructions through Joshua in verse 5:

> "Each of you is to take up a stone on his shoulder, according to the number of the tribes of the Israelites, to serve as a sign among you. In the future, when your children ask you, 'What do these stones mean?' tell them that the flow of the Jordan was cut off before the ark of the covenant of the Lord. When it crossed the Jordan, the waters of the Jordan were cut off. These stones are to be a memorial to the people of Israel forever."

This challenge from God to dads includes both building *and* telling.

Start a New Family Tradition: Tell Stories with Stones

Here is a way to bring this idea into the twenty-first century: **What if you started a tradition in your family where every time God did a big miracle**—like providing you the money to pay a huge bill or healing someone in a powerful way or answering a specific prayer or observing a milestone in your children's lives—**you took your kids to a quarry or a place that sells rocks and together picked out a sizable one to commemorate the event?** Then each time you bring one of these big rocks home, you can add it to a monument you're building in your yard where future generations will hear the stories that each rock tells. And through it all, dad, **you are the one leading the whole event,** just like the Israelite men of the Old Testament.

But let's not stop just yet with this theme of stones. We all know the story of David and Goliath. I think that being (and becoming) a great dad is a mammoth-sized task comparable to facing Goliath. **The task before you is *way* bigger than your resources.** Fathering is a daunting enterprise even on the best of days, and it undoubtedly overwhelms any guy who honestly faces this mission head on.

As you face the giant undertaking of being a dialed-in dad, like David, you come with a handful of "smooth stones" you've collected in your pocket. You've picked up things along your life journey for the task, and yet as you stand here *you are keenly aware that you are in over your head if you calculate your strength as a mere mortal.*

Your Strength Is in the God You Serve

In many ways you are in the best place possible if you can be honest about one thing: your strength and success as a dad isn't in *your power* or *your skills* or *your credentials* or *your wisdom*, but is in the God you serve. **You need a Power greater than yourself to equip you for the job.**

I imagine that you already are asking God daily for wisdom and strength to be a great dad. But if not, start today. And as you claim your spiritual authority in this role, you will be able to stand up against the enemy's attempts to derail you. I encourage you to write your prayers on note cards and put them in a prominent place to remind you daily to *ask*. James

4:2 says it this way, "You don't have what you want because you don't ask God for it" (NLT).

Admitting Weakness Is Strength

As a Father Himself, God understands what this role is like, so there's no better Person to ask help from. God says that it's *His* power that is made perfect in *our* weakness. When we admit that we don't have what we need to do the job, it's then that Christ's power can rest on us. The apostle Paul gives us a bold illustration of this when he shouts, "For when I am weak, then I am strong" (2 Corinthians 12:10).

It must have taken a big dose of courage for Paul to admit weakness since he was a rough and tumble, type A, mover-shaker-leader kind of guy. But if you follow his example, you will humbly lead your daughter and admit when you've hurt her. You will be willing to make amends afterward while laying down defensiveness. That is **humility in action**.

You have the opportunity today to follow in the footsteps of real men such as Joshua, David, and Paul who *stepped out* in *big* faith-filled ways while believing in a *big* God. **How incredible it would be to keep the legacy of great male leaders going strong in this generation.**

You, my friend, are building a legacy.

"I Can Live with Regret or I Can Live with Resolve"

I had a conversation recently at church with my longtime friend Dave, who is the father of five kids. Our conversation quickly went deep when, with tears in his eyes, he told me he really wants to be a great dad. I stood there tearing up alongside him as I saw the soft spot that led him to get emotional when talking about fatherhood. In describing his heart desire toward his fifteen-year-old daughter, Dave said, "In ten years she will be twenty-five. **I can either live with regret or I can live with resolve**. I get to decide now which one I want it to be."

Wow. I couldn't have said it any better. *Dave is a hero to me because he's taking action to pursue his daughter's heart.* He is joining the ranks of my biblical heroes, and you can too.

Let me sum up this chapter this way: It's up to you to decide what you want to do with the stones in your hand. You can either throw them (in anger) or you can use them to build a monument. I pray you are being inspired to intentionally build your legacy one stone at a time.

And once again, here are a few more introspective questions for you to consider as you evaluate your responses to your daughter with the goal of strengthening your relationship with her:

I know I threw a rock in anger and hit my daughter when...

My specific plan for making amends with her is (write a note, talk to her with no minimizing or excuses, take her on a date and humbly apologize while asking for forgiveness)...

The first miracle or milestone in our family that I'll be getting a rock to commemorate is...

CHAPTER 44

EARTHLY FATHER AND GOD THE FATHER

As we transition now from the earthly father-daughter relationship to our relationship with God the Father, here is a lens through which to evaluate these potential dynamics:

If your father was like this…		*You might see God like this…*
Flakey	F	**F**ake
Angry	A	**A**busive
Timid (passive)	T	**T**rustless
Hypocrite	H	**H**inderer
Empty (disengaged)	E	**E**lusive
Rigid	R	**R**ule-giver
If your father was like this…		*You might see God like this…*
Fair	F	**F**riend
Affectionate	A	**A**pproachable
Teachable	T	**T**rustworthy
Helpful	H	**H**ealer
Encouraging	E	**E**ngaged
Reliable	R	**R**eal

Clearly, this acrostic highlights the significance between your role as a dad and the way your daughter might respond to God as a Father. It may also help you understand the ways your own relationship with God has been shaped through interactions with your dad.

The conclusion that seems clear is this: *the horizontal lays the foundation for the vertical.*

Religious Influences Survey

Mark Holmen, in his book *Faith Begins at Home,* cites data from "The Most Significant Religious Influences Survey" by Search Institute of 3,121 teens between grades seven and twelve. I find the results noteworthy for a number of reasons:

- As a counselor and former youth leader, it surprises me that out of the twenty-eight people listed as influencers, "youth group leader at my church" is listed as number thirteen. That's saddening when you think of the hours youth leaders spend pouring into kids' lives.
- It's also interesting to me that "God in my life" is listed near the bottom (at number twenty-three) as a low influencer.
- With peer influence being central to teens, I was amazed to see that "friends" were as far down as number six, with "pastor" at number seven, and counselors not even on the list.

You'll Never Guess Who's #1 and #2

But guess who came out far and above the rest as the number one and number two most significant religious influencers to teens? **Mother was one and father was two.**

This survey implies that **regardless of the home a teen grows up in, mom and dad still have the most impact as religious and spiritual influencers.** And based on my experience, it also sadly resonates with me that dad ranks lower than mom in this role.

Why Aren't Dads Leading Spiritually?

Why do you think ***kids see dads as less significant spiritual leaders*** *than moms?*

- Could it be that women tend to take over because men aren't leading spiritually?
- Is it that church programs cater more to women than men, thus leading men to shy away from church involvement where they would gain tools to lead spiritually?
- Or could it be, as my friend David Murrow, author of *Why Men Hate Going to Church,* suggests, that men often see women as more skilled relationally and verbally, so when it comes to praying or being the spiritual leader, they tend to see their wives as better at these things and hold back?

Regardless of the reasons, when it comes to guiding your daughter's spirit, she needs *you* to lead because *you, dad, lay the foundation for how she relates to God the Father.* How's that for a weighty reality check?

Doing Nothing Is Doing It Wrong

Another big thing I take away from this survey is that no one else has as much spiritual impact on their kids as parents. This is where my passion for The Abba Project and equipping dads to lead more intentionally is rooted.

You don't have to be perfect at it. Just do something. I know you'd rather do nothing than to do it wrong, but if you do nothing in this area, then *that is doing it wrong.*

A Heartbroken Mom's Story

When I met Nancy at a conference, it didn't take long for her to pour out her heart to me once I told her that I lead dads of daughters. She said of her ex-husband and her daughter Hannah's dad that "he claims to believe in God, but he's been such a poor role model as a dad and it has done major damage in her life." This mom was truly grieving for her daughter.

Just the day before I met Nancy, she said that Hannah was cleaning her room and getting rid of things to send to Goodwill. Among them was a Bible her dad had given her a few years earlier when she graduated from high school. Inside the front cover he had written a note telling her that he hoped she could feel God's love through him. Clearly, it wasn't worth saving.

According to Nancy, Hannah "claims to be a Christian, but doesn't serve Him anymore." It's not surprising that this formerly treasured gift from her dad now had no value to her and was easy to cast aside, much like her faith.

After talking with me about the desperate need for dads to be more aware of their spiritual impact on their daughters, Nancy gave me the Bible and encouraged me to share this story. She believed this could be a redemptive thread in an otherwise heartbreaking story if it inspired other dads to grasp how important they are as a model of God the Father to their daughters.

Dad, live your life with conviction so that your daughter has a role model to follow. **Be the reason she turns to God the Father, not the reason she turns away.**

The reason I believe I'm holding back in spiritually leading my daughter is...

The area where I'm spiritually leading my daughter well is...

CHAPTER 45

EARTHLY FATHER AND GOD THE FATHER: THE GIRLS TELL ALL

I'm going to give you some practical tools in the next chapter, but first I want you to hear from girls in their teens and twenties on this issue of dads leading spiritually. And in a sincere desire not to stack the deck, you'll see that some of their responses don't exactly fit the survey I referenced earlier (about dad being a key spiritual influencer), yet still provide profound insights. For the record, I posed this question to girls of all faiths.

Question:

Do you see any obvious correlations between your dad's relationship with God, a Higher Power, or spirituality and his relationship with you?

"There are none because my dad actually talks, loves, and listens to God. This is sarcasm."

"Honestly, not really."

"I think that having a healthy and loving dad has definitely helped me have a healthy view of God."

"My father and I have never really talked about his views of religion. It is something he keeps very private, as do I, but overall I am thankful that my relationship with him is so great, and maybe some of that positive loyalty comes from his religion as well."

Daughters' Responses About Dad and Spiritual Influence

"Not that I can tell. He never talks about God with me. I know that he is devoted to his family and that he trusts in God."

"Obvious correlation? No. But I think he believes in a more judgmental God, and I can see that critical judgment at times. I think his determination of right and wrong has come from his strong religious background. Thankfully, those views have mellowed out. My dad has compassion for people and believes strongly in 'looking good,' which Catholicism preaches at times."

"He's Always Teaching Me New Things"

"Definitely. **I love how he leads me in being closer to God. It's definitely a place where we connect.** We both love to study the Bible and learn, so he's always teaching me new things."

"Absolutely. Because my dad loves the Lord and has found unconditional love from God (which he did not get as a child), **I know that he loves me unconditionally. I have never had to earn my love from my dad."**

"Yes, my dad 'plays' me and my sister as he does his higher power. He wants to convince us all that he is a good father, son, person, and it's because of that I don't fully trust him. The one thing that wakes him up in the morning and puts a smile on his face is his partner, not us [his two girls] and not god. And for the record, I don't have much of a connection with or need for god at this point in my life."

"*No*...I do not see a single correlation between my father's supposed 'relationship' with God and his 'relationship' with me."

"It's always been important to me that my dad influence my spiritual development. I still remember him reading Bible stories to me and my sister when we were little girls. I wish we had continued to have this intentional time together as I continued to grow, but somehow it eventually died off. I think my dad would be surprised to know how significant that was to me."

Spiritual Leadership from Dad Creates a Solid Foundation

I felt the passion and emotion as I read these responses, as I'm sure you did too. I heard their heart longings, especially when their dad wasn't spiritually intentional, resulting in their daughters not expecting much. By contrast, when dads did dial in spiritually, their daughters were grateful and expressed a desire for more.

As you read the following responses to one last question, *listen closely to these girls.* They are in the stages of life where their longings are clearer than anything I could say to you on their behalf.

What Practical Steps Can Dads Do?

Question:

What practical steps do you wish your dad would take to intentionally be the model and representation of God, a Higher Power, or spirituality to you?

"I like when my dad **calls me to let me know he's thinking of me or praying for me.** I really like praying together."

"I like when my dad **initiates anything related to spirituality,** like going to church together or going to a Christian concert."

"I like it when he **asks about my relationship with God or encourages me to pray.** There's something about a dad telling you to pray or spend time with God—it just hits you differently than if anyone else were to say the same thing."

"I would hope that my father would 'stop, look, and listen' to what he is portraying to others and myself. It's hard to give specifics when I feel my father is so far off base from what God is."

"I wish my dad was more open to other religions and was more interested in my spirituality and what I believe."

"Honestly, he needs to stop doing this exact thing. **Stop trying to be like God."**

"He already does work to bring me closer to God, which I love. I do wish that we could get more one-on-one time, just to talk through things that are going on in my life, questions that I have, emotions that I'm dealing with. I see that he gets that time with other people, but I wish I could have it too, and that it would be intentional."

"I wish my dad would have spent more time praying with my brother and me when we were younger. I knew he loved us and prayed for us, but it would have been great if it would have been a regular routine together. Overall, my dad is amazing, and I am so thankful that he is who he is."

"I wish he would bring up the subject with me, and ask about my spiritual heart."

"Ask About My Spiritual Heart"

"Honestly I don't know what I would change. He has been understanding and vulnerable about his own faith with me. He has loved me and modeled what God has in store for me."

"I accept where he is at this point in his life and do not expect him to show me how to be spiritual."

"To try and understand."

"It is something I must find on my own personal journey. For his sake, I do hope, however, that he learns to be more aware of others' feelings and tries to support a strong family union."

"I wish that he would ask me about my spiritual walk, and if I say I'm not doing well, I wish he would tell me how I can go about it. I also wish that he'd make an intentional effort to talk to me even when I'm really negative and upset, and that instead of brushing it off, he'd show that it matters and that he cares."

These are heartfelt, practical, vulnerable insights from daughters on what your spiritual investment as a dad means.

What If You're Not Her Hero Anymore?

Yet if, by any chance, you've made choices that have now resulted in a "fall from grace" in your daughter's eyes where you are no longer her hero or her "spiritual covering," there is still hope. I can tell you stories of dads who have made selfish, stupid choices or mistakes who later humbled themselves, admitted their wrongs, asked for forgiveness, and submitted to being held accountable. *Restoration and healing between these dads and daughters happened* after *dad engaged in his own recovery process.*

And finally, because I've spent a bit of time on Mars these past few years and am now "bilingual," I am fully aware of the need to use fewer words (which I admit has been a challenge for me throughout this book!). So I will now seek to summarize the key points of this chapter. (You're welcome.)

What a Daughter Needs Spiritually from Her Dad

(The Condensed Version)

- Pray *for* me.
- Pray *with* me.
- Ask me questions about my spiritual heart.
- Respond to my spiritual and life questions.
- Be vulnerable with me about your faith.
- Initiate conversations about God and spiritual things.

- Practice what you preach.
- Be intentional.
- Try to understand where I'm coming from.
- Create a spiritual routine with me.

Profound, wouldn't you say? I truly appreciate the vulnerability these insightful young women demonstrated, knowing that you as a dad would read them. The next chapter will include my thoughts on this theme, yet even if you stopped reading now, I believe you have been given the best advice right here from these daughters.

But first, by answering these next two questions, you will be ready to more effectively interact with your daughter on spiritual topics.

A question I have about spiritual things is...

What I will do more intentionally to lead and engage my daughter spiritually from this point on is...

CHAPTER 46

PRACTICAL ADVICE FOR LEADING YOUR DAUGHTER SPIRITUALLY

Dad, I realize I may be treading on sacred ground here as I provide you with suggestions about what it means to be a spiritual influence in your daughter's life. Please understand that I approach this subject with the greatest of respect because spiritual beliefs and practices are a very personal, often private thing. The ideas I propose here are based on my experience, as well as firsthand information from girls who have shared what they want and need spiritually from their dads.

And because of my commitment to help equip you to dial in to your daughter, I would be remiss if I didn't address the spiritual realm as much as the emotional and relational realms. I also know it can all be a bit overwhelming and daunting. So I suggest that you *choose one area in my baker's dozen list and start there.* Here are some practical things that you can begin doing *today* in order to engage your daughter spiritually.

Choose One Area and Start Today

The Baker's Dozen for Leading Spiritually

1. **Let her see you engaging in your own spiritual practices.** You all know the saying: *More is caught than taught.*
2. **Pray with her about things going on in her life.** This means you're asking her about her life, boys, school, work, commitments, friends, and activities.
3. **Write out a prayer for her in a note, a text, or an email.**
4. **Tell her what God is doing in your life. Talk about answers to your prayers.**

5. **Open up about what you're learning from the Bible or spiritual book or study.** But not in a way that preaches at her or has hidden statements to convict her. This is about you sharing what *you* are gleaning spiritually in your own life.
6. **Share how God is convicting you.** This one may be harder to be open about and one where discretion obviously is warranted. But if you let your daughter know how God is speaking to you, modeling the fact that you are listening and responding, this will go farther than any lecture you can ever give her.
7. **Reveal your own questions about spiritual things.** Let her know you have questions about God, the Bible, theology, church practices, and other matters while demonstrating that asking questions is normal and healthy. Find answers to her questions and make it a fun, creative process to search for answers together, as well as on your own. Report back on what you find.
8. **Ask her what she believes.** Listen, learn, and no lectures. Ask questions to draw her out without necessarily sharing your beliefs at first. If talking about spiritual things is new, it may take a while for her to open up honestly. Wisely choose your words and take an interest in her beliefs and look through her eyes. Seek to understand her.
9. **Go to a Christian concert with her** by one of her favorite artists and then each share what it was like for you.
10. **Attend her church with her or invite her to yours.** Talk about the sermon and the things you gleaned from it. Ask questions about what touched her or spoke to her.
11. **Sing worship songs with her and listen to the lyrics that touch her spirit.** Talk about why they have meaning. (You don't have to sing well to do this; focus on sharing the moment.)
12. **Ask her to share with you about a spiritually significant time in her life.** Then share one of yours.
13. **Buy her a book on a spiritual theme.** Read it with her. Discuss what you both learn.

Word Association Game

Next, I'd like to give you another way to approach this theme from the standpoint of understanding our brains and how we encode information. We'll do this by playing a game called "word association."

Word association is a method of understanding what is already in someone's brain (while revealing the meaning attached) by having that person state the first thing that comes to mind when they hear a prompted word. To demonstrate this, I'm going to give you a word and I'd like you to say the first thing that comes to mind when you hear it. Here goes:

Water.

What words immediately come to your mind upon seeing that word *water*? I'm guessing you thought of words like *thirst* or *refreshing* or *bathe* or *shower.*

Now I'll ask the question in a slightly different way. If you lived in Sendai, Japan, during the magnitude 9.0 earthquake and powerful tsunami on March 11, 2011, what words would instantly come to mind when you heard the word *water*? I imagine words like *death, terror, loss, tragedy,* and *devastation* would come readily to mind.

Here's my third question in this word association game: What words come to mind when you hear the word *father*?

You may have answered *protector, teacher, friend,* or *provider.* Or you may have answered with words like *absent, abusive, workaholic, harsh,* or *disinterested.*

Words Tie to Our Individual and Unique History

I'm sure you can see where I'm going with this. We associate words and themes with our history. In fact, it is only from what we have experienced that we have an understanding of people, concepts, beliefs, events, places, and on it goes.

That is why, when it comes to God the Father, we all reference Him, the Unseen, through what we have experienced and lived, the seen. And in this case, dad, what is seen is *you.*

You may be doing a really great job of being consistent, trustworthy, and intentional with your daughter, thus modeling God the Father to her in a positive way. On the other hand, you may be a dad who has misrepresented God in a way that has caused her harm. Despite the way you have fathered your daughter, here is the truth I want to shout from the rooftops: **Whether you had the best dad in the world or whether you have been the best dad in the world, we all need more than a father can give.**

We All Need More Than a Father Can Give

Your Father in heaven is turned toward you and is the Perfect Dad, the only One who can give you what you need and long for. Only He can heal the depths of your heart and the depths of your hurt.

An earthly dad can do his best, but because he is a flawed human being, even on the best of days he (or you) can't heal everything. **But the love of a dad goes a long way toward healing a girl's heart.** That much I know for sure.

But what do you do if you as a dad didn't get this? Do you think it's possible that if an earthly dad is our "greatest untapped natural resource" for emotional healing that a close relationship with *God the Father* could be our greatest untapped resource for spiritual healing?

I'm sure by now you know that my answer is *yes.*

Spiritual Muscle Training

And if you want to do more in-depth *spiritual muscle training,*

- Begin by looking up the word *Father* (and *Abba*) in a Bible concordance or pull up a Bible app on your smartphone.
- Write out every single Bible verse on fathering, as well as the truths you discover about God the Father. (My friend, Dr. Ken Canfield has counted 1190 biblical references to fathers/fathering in the Bible. There is rich soil on this topic if you start digging. To get you started, I would suggest looking at Deuteronomy 1:30-31, Psalm 103:13, Zephaniah 3:17, Matthew 7:9-11, and 1 John 3:1).
- Turn those truths into a prayer so that you have the Ultimate Father guiding and leading you to be the best dad you can be to your daughter.

A Prayer You Can Pray

Here is a sample prayer you can pray if these words capture the longing of your heart to be God's man in your role as a father:

> *Dear Abba Father God,*
>
> *I know that You are the perfect Father, One who gives and consistently loves, One who disciplines with grace and mercy, One who always protects while doing what is best for Your children. Though my heart's longing ever since my daughter was born has been to be the best dad in the world, I see how often I fall short. I need Your help and wisdom.*
>
> *Please speak to me when I am wrong so that I can humble myself and quickly make it right with my daughter. Quicken me with awareness before I respond in anger so that I don't squelch her spirit. Soften me so that I can gently interact with her. Equip me to lead*

with loving strength. Guide me to actively build her up rather than tear her down so that my words and attitudes and interactions breathe life into her. And when I do need to confront or set boundaries or discipline, empower me to do it without being harsh...as You do with me.

Thank You for modeling to me the role of a loving Father, One who never gives up and never rejects. Thank You for never turning Your back on me or making me grovel for Your attention, favor, or love. Keep me on my face before You, willing to be broken while admitting my need for You.

I know that without Your ever-present help and guidance, I will fail and fall short of being a true model and representative of You to my daughter. I want to make You known to her, and I can do this only in Your strength and with Your power. Help me, Abba Father God.

I give You permission to lead me, convict me, and love through me. Thank You in advance for the answers to my prayer.

Challenge: Pray This for 21 Days

If this prayer reflects the desire of your heart, I encourage you to pray it daily for twenty-one days. Experts say that it takes that long to make something a habit. Why not challenge yourself to repeat this prayer for three entire weeks and see what kind of impact it has on the way you parent.

And if you have stories to tell, I'd love you to share them with me by writing me at *michelle@theabbaproject.com.* I'm here to celebrate the victories and milestones with you.

You Can't Always Be There, but Her Abba Father Can

Your daughter needs you to lead her to a Power and Resource *greater* than herself and *greater* than you so that when she is struggling and you're not around, she can tap into God's strength and help.

Lead her to her ultimate Source of life.

It's time for another dad-daughter date. This one will open up dialogue on the key topic of spiritual issues. *Lead with courage.* See the appendix for **"Date 8: Dad to Daughter Questions on Spiritual Issues."**

CHAPTER 47

SPIRITUAL WRAP-UP: THE END IS THE BEGINNING

Here we are at the *end* of our journey together. But this is just the *beginning* of what I hope and pray will be a change in you as you more ***intentionally*** and ***consistently*** pursue your daughter's heart.

Speaking of endings, when you read a book or watch a movie, do you give much significance to the ending? Of course you do.

A Good Ending Gives Closure and Perspective

There is nothing worse for a moviegoer than a movie that leaves you hanging. By contrast, a good ending not only wraps up the loose ends of a story, but it puts things in perspective. I've found that it always pays to stay tuned until the very end because that's when the story comes together.

Another kind of ending, one that is more sobering, is the end of someone's life. In those last moments, every second is savored and cherished by those gathered around. Everyone is in highly attentive mode, perhaps more so than at any other time. Every word or glance or interaction has extra significance because those interactions will soon be ending.

With that backdrop, let me ask another question: Do you know the very last verse of the Old Testament? Until a couple of years ago I couldn't have answered that question either. However, I now believe it's one of the most significant verses in all the Bible.

The Last Statement Before God Signed Off for a While

This statement had to have been *extraordinary* and *extra significant* because God knew He was "signing off" for the next four hundred years. So I'm not the only one who thinks endings are noteworthy. God does too.

Here is what God said in the last two verses of the entire Old Testament: "Look, I am sending you the prophet Elijah before the great and dreadful day of the Lord arrives. His preaching will turn the hearts of fathers to their children, and the hearts of children to their fathers. Otherwise I will come and strike the land with a curse" (Malachi 4:5-6 NLT).

How's that for intense? A curse just because dads and kids aren't turned toward each other? Seems kind of harsh, doesn't it?

The placement here in the Bible wasn't random. God was purposeful in His choice of where to put those carefully chosen words. His extremely powerful statement was left ringing in the ears of His people as He bid them adieu for the next four centuries.

Dads and Kids Are a Big Deal to God

And though it may have seemed that God would have had more important things to focus on than dads and kids—things like His relationship with mankind, Jesus coming to save the world, and even about heaven and hell—yet apparently this *was* the topic most pressing on His heart.

Conclusion: **This dad-child thing is a big deal to God.**

The end of Malachi is the beginning of understanding how important the dad-child relationship is to God's heart. Let me say it another way: God was highlighting the fact that *the hearts of fathers were (and still are) a key influence on the hearts and lives of their children.*

I thought it was worth wrapping up our journey together in the same way that Abba Father God closed out the Old Testament: *With a challenge to fathers.*

Time to Turn, Restore, Change, or Convince Your Daughter of Your Love

Let's dig deeper into this challenge. God used the word *turn* when speaking of the action He was challenging dads to take. This implies that their hearts had been leaning in the opposite direction and God was calling for a directional change. The word translated *turn* has many facets:

- *Restore*, meaning to rebuild and repair
- *Change*, which underscores, in this context, the movement in a dad's attitude toward his children and his children's attitudes toward him
- *Convince*, involving demonstration and providing evidence for a course of action

I am *convinced* that the *turning* of hearts (dads *and* their kids) will occur if a dad works on his relationships with his kids, resulting in a *change of direction and restoration.*

Now let's look at the last part of the verse where God says: *"If they [dads and children] refuse, I'll come and put the land under a curse"* (MSG).

Some believe these words refer to the generation during Malachi's time that was walking in disobedience to God. Their rebellious choices led God to warn them that if they failed to repent and turn to Him, then Jesus's coming would prove to be a curse. Others believe this warning has to do with the possibility that God would use surrounding nations to invade and destroy the nation of Israel.

When I think of that last interpretation, I can't help but wonder what antagonists in the twenty-first century attempt to overpower and destroy girls. What potential curses could come against a daughter if her dad's heart isn't turned toward her? What is it that hits at the core of a girl's life and attempts to attack, overpower, and extinguish the person she is?

I believe there are two kinds of threats to any nation or person: *internal* and *external*. Here are a few of my thoughts about what I consider to be potential threats to a girl's heart:

External threats:

1. Other girls (If you've never seen the movie *Mean Girls*, it's worth watching just to capture the brutal intensity of girls trying to navigate life with other girls.)
2. Guys
3. Rejection
4. Drivenness to perform, produce, succeed

And then there are ***internal threats:***

5. Drug or alcohol addictions
6. Eating disorders
7. Negative body image
8. Low self-esteem
9. Premarital sex (I list this as an internal threat because most girls wrestle internally with this decision even though peer pressure or other external influences may be involved.)

External Threats to Her Heart Health

Internal Threats to Her Heart Health

A Dad-Shaped Vacuum Only You Can Fill

You've probably heard the famous saying that "we all have a God-shaped vacuum that only He can fill." Similarly, I believe that **every girl has a dad-shaped vacuum that only her dad can fill**.

Dads are called by God to stand in the gap and fight for their kids. As a dad intentionally invests in his daughter's life, his action will directly counter the internal and external threats against her, resulting in subsequent decreases in:

Here's What You'll Have to Show for Your Investment

- drug and alcohol use or abuse (*because there will be less need to numb*)
- eating disorders (*because there will be less need to control*)
- negative body image (*because her dad will model to her more self-acceptance and grace*)
- low self-esteem (*because she will have more confidence and embrace her full potential since she has her dad backing her and believing in her*)
- premarital sex (*because there will be less looking for "love" in all the wrong places since her love tank is already being filled in a legitimate and healthy way*)

Because God emphasized the father-child relationship at the end of the first part of His book, I figure it's an important point to emphasize in mine. But it's up to you to choose to invest like never before.

You Have a God-Given Assignment

You as a dad have the God-given assignment to engage your daughter's heart by turning toward her and inviting her to do the same. You have to make the first move. She'll come toward you if you are loving, gentle, and kind. She needs your love expressed consistently, intentionally, positively, and softly.

So here, at the end of this journey, give yourself one last challenge by writing in the box a response *for yourself*. Remember you are doing this for yourself out of love for your daughter.

The title of this book is *Dad, Here's What I Really Need from You.* What I know for sure that my daughter really wants and needs from me as her dad is...

Please hear my heart in saying that I applaud you for being willing to enter into this process out of love for your daughter. You can change history (her story and yours) by intentionally *kicking it up a notch* in pursuit of your daughter's heart.

You Can Change History

Thank you for the privilege of allowing me to walk alongside you through this maze of becoming a more dialed-in dad. Thank you for putting up with my Venusian wordiness and making it here to the end. I truly mean it when I say that I want to hear your stories—the good, the bad, and the ugly. You can send those to *michelle@theabbaproject.com*.

Finally, **never underestimate your role in your daughter's life. Make every day count.**

And now that you know what your daughter *really* needs from you, *keep your heart turned toward hers, and you both will thrive.*

APPENDIX

A GUIDE FOR DAD-DAUGHTER DATES

Date 1: Dad to Daughter Questions

This first date questionnaire is light and fun.

- Plan a lunch or coffee date with your daughter and use these questions to get to know her in this season of her life.
- As you begin this dialogue, allow yourself to really listen to her responses without teaching or directing the conversation.
- Let her know there will be no criticism of her answers because you are here to build a stronger relationship with her. This is about getting to know her for who she is. And remember that you play a vital role in mirroring the truth about the girl she is and the woman she is becoming.
- The majority of these questions are lighthearted in order to set a solid relational foundation with open communication here from the start.

Let's begin with things in the present and work our way back, then forward. I know there are a lot of questions so feel free to choose your **top five favorites** in each section…and have fun!

Present

1. What item of my clothing would you love to see me get rid of?
2. What things about me make you laugh?
3. Tell me something I do that embarrasses you.

4. Who is your favorite band right now?
5. What is your favorite song right now? (Ask her to tell you some of the lyrics and explain why she likes them. If she has her iPod with her, ask to listen to the song…and remember: no criticism. Listen to understand her thoughts about the song.)
6. What is your favorite food and least favorite food right now?
7. What is your favorite item(s) of clothing right now?
8. What is your favorite class and least favorite class right now?
9. Is there any way I can support you with any class that you are struggling with?
10. Tell your daughter what your best and worst subjects were in school (share in brief since this is about drawing her out).
11. What do you look for in a guy? (This may seem embarrassing for her to disclose to you, but hang in there and encourage her to tell you her thoughts.)
12. What bugs you about guys?
13. What is your favorite TV show right now? What do you like about it?
14. Is there anything you wish we would do, either as a family or just the two of us, that would have meaning to you?
15. In what ways do you think we're alike and in what ways do you think we're different?
16. What do you think is good and not good about our relationship right now? (Remember that at this stage in the journey you can ask this question, but it's best to keep it light and allow her space to comment if she so chooses.)
17. Tell your daughter one or two physical characteristics that you find beautiful about her (girls remember these kinds of affirmations from their dads).

Past

1. What is one of your favorite childhood memories?
2. What was one of your favorite childhood toys? (Then you can tell her about one of your favorite childhood toys as well.)

3. What is or has been your favorite holiday and why?
4. What traditions from that holiday are your favorite, where just thinking about them brings a smile and makes you happy?
5. When you think about our relationship through the years, when do you remember us being the closest?
6. On a scale of 0 to 10, with 10 being the most and 0 being neutral, how close would you say we are now?
7. Tell me about a memory of you and me that means a lot to you. (Then you can share a memory of the two of you that you also hold close to your heart.)
8. Can you think of a time when you remember me being there for you that still comes to mind as a positive memory? (Share a positive memory with her that you also have of the two of you.)
9. *Optional*: Does any specific memory stand out where I really blew it with you, misunderstood you, or wasn't there for you? (Since this beginning exercise is about bridge-building, this question may be best saved for later, but you know your daughter and can decide if it's best to talk openly like this today.)

Future

1. Do you ever think about your wedding day? If so, what do you imagine? What colors do you want? What will your dress look like? What setting do you picture? If not, what about a wedding doesn't appeal to you? (Remember that most girls have been dreaming about and planning their weddings since they were little girls, so this most likely is something she'll easily talk about.)
2. If there were no limits in any way and you could be anyone you wanted to be, do anything you wanted to do, or go anywhere you wanted to go, what would that look like for you?
3. What do you think would make our relationship better this next year?
4. Are there times you feel I could improve on listening to and understanding you?

5. Is there anything you think I could improve on in my parenting of you? (Remind her that this isn't a question about how you parent any of your other kids, this is just about you and her. This might be a scary question to ask, but if you listen without being defensive, it can open up great dialogue.)
6. *Optional*: Is there any question you would like to ask me?

End by affirming your love for your daughter, letting her know that you are grateful she is your daughter and that you want to know her more as she grows and changes and matures.

Date 2: Dad to Daughter Questions on Self-Esteem

These questions are on self-esteem. You can start by reading the scripted questions out loud to her on your date. And if she does better in writing, give her the questions prior to your date and ask her to bring them with her.

> *"Hi Honey...I've been learning some things about self-esteem, which is the term used to describe how someone feels about themselves. I'd love to hear more about what you're thinking and feeling about yourself in this season of life."*

Remember that if you share answers to these questions and open up about yourself, she won't feel like she's on the hot seat.

1. What three words would you use to best describe yourself lately?
2. On a scale of 0 to 10, with 0 being low and not good and 10 being high and great, what number would you say best captures how you feel about yourself these days?
3. On a scale of 0 to 10, with 0 being low and not good and 10 being high and great, what number would you say captures how you felt about yourself a year ago?
4. What has affected your view of yourself (going up or down) this past year?
5. It's been said that "the more worthy a girl feels of having good things happen to her, the better she feels about herself and the world around her."
    - Do you feel like you're worthy enough to have good things happen to you?

- Do you ever blame yourself when bad things happen to you or around you?

"I'd love to hear more about what you just said if you'd like to share more about it with me. I know it's hard being a girl, and I'd love to have you teach me about what things are like for you."

6. They say that many things influence self-esteem, including personality, physical appearance, emotions and emotional health, abilities, habits, and morality.
   - What do you like and not like about your personality?
   - What abilities do you have that you're proud of?
   - What do you like and not like about your physical appearance?
   - What habits do you have that you like and what habits do you not like?
   - What morals do you have that you're proud of? Are there any you're not proud of?

7. Can you help me know how I can come alongside you and support you in feeling better about yourself? You can write me a letter if that would be easier for you than telling me right now.

Date 3: Dad to Daughter Questions on Words

As you'll notice, the topics are beginning to go deeper into places inside herself where she holds emotions and beliefs. This date is about words you've spoken that have stuck with her.

1. What are some of your favorite memories about specific words that I've spoken to you that have had meaning and value to you?
2. Can you think of a time or times when I said something to you that hurt you and has stayed with you and replayed in your head? What did I say? I promise that I won't get mad or defensive. I really want to know so I can make it right.
3. How did my words cause you to feel about yourself?
4. Can you think of a time or times when I failed to say something to you that you wished I would have said that has

stayed with you and replayed in your head? What did I not say that has stayed with you and replayed in your head?

5. If this reflects your heart, tell your daughter: "I admit that I don't always talk to you in ways that truly reflect my heart of love for you, and sometimes I react to you more than respond. But my heart desire is to invest in you in ways that build you up rather than tear you down."

Date 4: Write a Letter to Your Daughter

Girls appreciate having a break from answering hard questions, so the preparation for this date is all yours. You will write a letter to your daughter before the date and then read it to her in person (if possible) so she can hear your tone and read your body language.

The beauty of putting your thoughts, feelings, dreams, and love for your daughter into written form is so she can read and reread your letter. She will treasure the things you write to her both now and for years to come.

Here are some ideas about what you can include:

- What was one of the things you remember about her when you saw her for the very first time?
- What beauty did you see in her then and what beautiful features do you see in her now? (Girls love hearing about their eyes, smile, features that resemble their mother or grandmother, even their hands. Especially for girls with eating disorders, these features tend to be more neutral and therefore easier to respond to and hear positively.)
- Write about a favorite childhood memory you have of her.
- What do you believe her strengths are, both in her skills and in her person (her character, personality)?
- Tell her where exactly you're proud of her—her "who" (on the inside) and her "do" (the things she does).
- Write about what obstacles you have seen her overcome (emphasize such qualities as courage, resilience, strength, commitment, endurance, power).
- Write about dreams you have for her future, whether in the form of your wishes for her or supporting her dreams.
- Tell her things you pray about for her.

- Tell her what it's meant to you to have dates with her more regularly lately.
- Let her know that you will always be there for her, telling her what it means to you to be her dad.
- Include the meaning of her name and let her know how you see her embodying that meaning. You can look up the meaning of her name online as there are many websites that provide that information. I have yet to meet a girl who doesn't come alive once she finds out what her name means. It gives her a piece of her identity that is woven into the fiber of who she is. Your letter can applaud that truth.

Date 5: Dad to Daughter Questions on Seeing Herself and Body Image

The questions for this date are intended to help you understand how your daughter sees herself, coupled with questions about body image since these themes often accompany each other.

> *"Hi Honey... I want to better understand how you see yourself and especially how you see your body image. I'd like you to answer honestly, and I promise that I won't get defensive. I want to hear your honest answers so I can be more sensitive to you."*

1. Does the way I see you impact the way you see yourself? If so, then how? If not, why not?
2. Does my view of you impact you more, less, or the same as other people's view of you?
3. How about in comparison to guys? Whose reflection of you matters most, a guy's or mine? Be honest.
4. What do you need more of from me regarding how I see you?
5. How does my reflection of you now differ from when you were younger? Is it less or more important now compared to when you were five, ten, fifteen, or ______________?
6. The whole concept of body image is one that we guys don't tend to think about much. Can you help me understand how your image of your body affects you each day (such as your mood, thoughts, feelings, and choices about what to wear)?
7. What part(s) of your body do you like the best?
8. What part(s) of your body do you have a hard time accepting?

I'm not trying to embarrass you. I'm just trying to understand you better so I can be more sensitive to you in the areas where you're most sensitive about your body.

9. What have you learned about body image from watching me and your mom?
10. What comments to you about your body have stuck with you, whether positive or negative? These may be things said by me, someone in our family, a friend. I know it's not true that "sticks and stones may break my bones but words will never hurt me." Words do stay with us, and I wonder if you replay in your mind any negative statements or criticisms that have hurt you. Can you tell me more about this?
11. With this final point, I want you to hear my voice in your head so it replays and lets you know how much I adore you. When I look at you, I see…

Date 6: Dad to Daughter Questions on Romance and Royalty

The questions for this date are on romance and royalty. Some of this may not be her thing and that's okay. The important thing is to open up dialogue with her as you listen to her thoughts.

> *"Hi Honey…I know this theme of royalty and romance is one that I, as your dad, would never think of focusing on. I guess it's a men-are-from-Mars-women-are-from-Venus thing. I'd love to hear your thoughts and learn how to better pursue your heart by hearing what you have to say."*

1. Do you remember as a little girl liking to dress up as a princess? If so, tell me about it. If you didn't enjoy that, why not?
2. As a little girl (or even now) were you drawn to movies (especially Disney movies) about princesses? I'd love to hear about which characters you liked and why you liked them. (This is a time to reminisce on princesses or characters she used to connect with when she was a little girl.)
3. Now that you're older (and as silly as it may sound), do you ever think anymore about being a princess? If you did bring "the princess" back into your life, how would it affect you?

4. What messages about being a girl and being pretty or beautiful did you get from the movies you watched then (or now)?
5. How do the themes of being a princess (royalty) and being romanced tie together in your mind? Or do they?
6. If you are okay sharing it, what are your dreams and thoughts about what romance looks like? Be as honest as you can even if your wishes seem out of the realm of possibility.
7. Have you ever had a guy romance you in that way?
8. Can you think of any ways that I could make you feel more like royalty, like a princess?
9. If I were to fill up your love tank by making you feel loved and special and accepted and enjoyed, what could I do specifically to make you feel those things now?

Date 7: Dad to Daughter Questions on Guys, Dating, and Relationships

Some of these topics and questions may be hard to talk about, but if you don't weigh in on this subject, then every other voice will speak into her life except yours.

> *"Hi Honey. . . I'd love for us to have an open and real talk about guys, dating, and relationships. This isn't an area that dads and daughters tend to talk about, but you and I can be trendsetters. I really do want to understand what you think about these things even if it's a bit uncomfortable and new for both of us. Are you in?"*

1. Who are some of your favorite guys in movies, on TV, or in music (past or present)?
2. What do you like about them?
3. What qualities do you look for in a guy that you would date?
4. What qualities do you dislike in a guy?
5. In your view, what is the worst thing a guy could ever do to a girl?
6. Do you know any guys who would ever do that? (Or have you heard of any guys who have done that even if not to you?)

7. What is one of the best dates you've ever been on? (If she hasn't dated yet, ask her what her perfect date would look like.)
8. What is one of the worst dates you've ever been on (or could imagine going on)?
9. When you think of your friends, how many of them are in what you would call a "good relationship"?
10. In your view, what makes a relationship good? What makes a relationship bad?
11. Why do you think girls stay in relationships with guys past the point where it doesn't feel right to them anymore?
12. What is the yuckiest thing a guy has ever done to you? Would you be willing to tell me about it—even if just a part of it?
13. Have I ever been hurtful or insensitive to you about guys or dating?
14. What would make it easier to talk to me about guys and dating?
15. What do you wish I would do more to invest in your heart?
16. What do you like or not like about me taking you on dates?
17. Is there anywhere we could go or something you'd like to do with me that would make you feel special and loved by me?
18. Is there anything you want to ask me about what dating was like for me when I was your age?
19. Here's a list of needs that I've heard girls have. If you were to list your three most important needs, which would they be?

    - seen (noticed)
    - heard (listened to)
    - communicated with/talked with (she needs words)
    - desired (wanted)
    - pursued (this confirms her worth)
    - adored (made to feel special, important, unique)
    - enjoyed (laughed with, had fun with)

- respected (valued)
- loved (treasured)
- esteemed (honored)

Close by thanking her for her honesty and letting her know you will be her number one guy through thick and thin.

Date 8: Dad to Daughter Questions on Spiritual Issues

Your daughter may have different spiritual or religious views than you. The important thing is to open up dialogue, listen, and learn about what she thinks and believes. Seek to keep this nonconfrontational while focusing on understanding her better, being willing to share some of what you believe as well.

> *"Hi Honey…I'm learning that my relationship with you influences the way you see or relate to God or think about spiritual things. I want to be a positive role model for you spiritually even if we're on different pages. I could use your help to better understand where you're at spiritually and also hear from you about how I can be a stronger spiritual influence in your life."*

1. What adjectives would you use to describe your relationship with me?
2. From what you can tell, what kind of relationship (or lack of) do you think I have with God?
3. Do you see any obvious correlations between my relationship with God and my relationship with you?
4. I'd like to hear where you're at these days spiritually. No judgment or criticism, just open and honest dialogue. From your vantage point, do you and I hold to the same spiritual perspectives or practices? What are your thoughts on our similarities and differences?
5. Do I influence your spiritual side or does that seem irrelevant or unimportant to you? I'd like to hear specifics on whether my influence or lack of influence matters to you.
6. Do you have any questions about my faith?
7. How do Mom and I differ in how we spiritually relate to you, talk with you, and model this part of our lives to you?
8. What have you learned about relating to God as Father or

about connecting (or not connecting) with your spiritual side from watching me?

9. What do you believe my strengths are in modeling God or spirituality to you? In what ways am I a poor model of God or spirituality to you? I know this will probably be hard to answer, but I want to hear your thoughts on this. If it's easier to write it down, then that's fine with me as well.
10. What practical steps do you wish I'd take to be the model, leader, and representation of God or spirituality to you?
11. Is there anything I haven't asked about your spiritual life that you'd like me to know?
12. Do you have any questions regarding spiritual issues or anything I can pray about for you or talk about with you right now?

ACKNOWLEDGMENTS

As we all know, every story has a backstory. The backstory that has brought this book to life has me writing this sentence with tears of gratitude filling my eyes. Although you see one name, my name, on the cover of this book, myriads of human angels have graced me with kindness throughout this entire project. Thank you to each of you for joining me in my happy dance as we celebrate the birthing of this "baby"!

I begin first by thanking Terry Glaspey of Harvest House for believing in me when we started this conversation three years ago at Opryland. Coupled with your editorial genius, you are forever woven into the fiber of these pages.

Rod Morris, thank you for spending countless hours taking my first attempt at authorship and transforming it, somehow making me sound better than I actually am. As a seasoned editor, your gift as a wordsmith has brought clarity and precision to this project.

Thank you, Harvest House Publishers, for taking a leap of faith in aligning with me, a first-time author, as we partner to put tools into the hands of fathers across our country so they can succeed in pursuing their daughters' hearts.

Sandra Bishop, as my agent you share a passion for seeing healing in father-daughter relationships. Thank you for supporting the need along with me.

Jan and Jim Watson, my selfless and generous parents, who together have been my lifelong backbone of strength. Mom, thank you for filling myriads of prayer journals and interceding for me every single day while faithfully modeling what it looks like to be a vibrant woman of God who grows more beautiful with age. And Dad, you have lovingly and consistently been "my main man" from day one. Thank you for being involved in every aspect of my life, from being my number one supporter of The Abba Project to mowing my lawn just the way I like it to our Monday night Costco dates where you join me in taking silly pictures in the aisles. The two of you make my life more fun and balanced. I love you dearly.

Abba Project Dads, your numbers grow with each passing year, and without your participation, I wouldn't have this book or this ministry. Each of you inspires me as I see your willingness to invest intentionally in pursuing your daughters' hearts while locking arms as a band of brothers who challenge each other in the process. Thank you for allowing me the privilege of speaking into your lives. I am humbled and grateful beyond what mere words can express. Thank you, Clay Swanson, for being a steady, humble, godly man in your role as my coleader and friend.

My prayer team, all sixty of you, have immeasurable value to me and to the heart of The Abba Project. Without your loving intercession, I would be carrying things alone. Thank you for consistently pressing into God's throne and asking for miracles on my behalf. Together you are a mighty force and a precious gift to me.

Constance Rhodes, as a mover and shaker, visionary, and enthusiastic connector of people, your continual support of me from the first time we met years ago has led me to where I am today. Your love for prayer and your faith to believe for greater things inspires me.

Connie Patty, my best friend of thirty-five years, you have celebrated life with me even from halfway across the globe. Your fervent prayer life, hunger for the Word, and your love for your God and your family, all the while living surrendered to the Father's will, is something I respect and adore about you. Your book is next.

Bo Stern, my faith-filled, vulnerable friend, you are one of the most passionate Jesus followers I know. Thank you for encouraging me and for being available to answer my myriads of writing questions, all the while modeling what faith on the battlefield really looks like.

Dr. Ken Canfield, you are an incredible combination of humble strength and stellar leadership. I am in awe of the way God uses you. And then somehow, in the midst of impacting fathers around the globe, you have made time to be my friend. Thank you for challenging me and teaching me, especially when it comes to understanding how biblical fathering reflects the Father heart of God.

Dr. Jim Friesen, my mentor and true heart friend, you remind me so much of Jesus in the way you take complicated truths and make them practical. I love Jesus more because of the gracious, kind way you represent Him to me.

And I've saved the best for last. I give all glory and honor to my Abba Father, Jesus, and Holy Spirit for their redemptive, healing work in my life that has restored this broken jar of clay. Without them I would have nothing to say or write about. My deepest desire is to honor them with every fiber of my being. Thank You, Trinity, for allowing me a small piece in Your bigger work.